MW01100287

Revisiting
Racialized
Voice

Revisiting Racialized Voice

African American
Ethos in Language and
Literature

DAVID G. HOLMES

Southern Illinois University Press
Carbondale

Copyright © 2004 by the Board of Trustees,
Southern Illinois University
All rights reserved
Printed in the United States of America

Chapter 6, "The Rhetoric of Black Voice: Implications for Composition Pedagogy," is based on "Fighting Back by Writing Black: Beyond Racially Reductive
Composition Theory," by David G. Holmes, in *Race, Rhetoric, and Composition*,
edited by Keith Gilyard. Published by Boynton/Cook Publishers, a subsidiary of
Reed Elsevier, Inc., Portsmouth, NH, 1999.

Library of Congress Cataloging-in-Publication Data
Holmes, David Glen.
Revisiting racialized voice : African American ethos in language and literature /
David G. Holmes.
    p. cm.
Includes bibliographical references and index.
    1. African Americans—Languages. 2. American literature—African American
authors—History and criticism. 3. English language—Rhetoric—Study and teach-
ing—United States. 4. Dialect literature, American—History and criticism. 5. Af-
rican Americans—Education—Language arts. 6. African Americans in literature.
7. Race in literature. 8. Black English. I. Title.
PE3102.N42 H65 2004
810.9'896073—dc21   2003012598
ISBN 0-8093-2547-0 (alk. paper)

Printed on recycled paper. ♻

The paper used in this publication meets the minimum requirements of American
National Standard for Information Sciences—Permanence of Paper for Printed
Library Materials, ANSI Z39.48-1992. ∞

For James E. Smythe,
who saw my potential to be a scholar before I could

Contents

Preface

THERE HAS BEEN MUCH DISCUSSION ABOUT RACE and voice in composition studies, from the emergence of "The Students' Right to Their Own Language" in 1974 until the present. The field of rhetoric and composition has also produced a number of significant works that explore the rich history of African American oratory and literacy, Shirley Wilson Logan's *"We Are Coming,"* Jacqueline Jones Royster's *Traces of a Stream,* and Bradford T. Stull's *Amid the Fall,* to name just a few.

In this book, I begin reexamining both the ideological and interdisciplinary relationships among literature, oratory, and composition epitomized in an explication of the metaphor of black voice. My specific contribution will be twofold. First, I will contribute to the discussion about the racialization of voice from the 1870s through the 1920s (chapters 1 and 2). Second, I will trace through representative authors the evolution of black voice from its literal use to its metaphorical use, first in literature and then, by extension, in composition (chapters 3–6).

My overall purpose is to afford African American students more flexibility in constructing their own racialized ethos in writing. Many African American authors have fought for such flexibility, particularly during the 1870s through the 1920s. Many such writers and, more to the point, student writers continue to fight for this flexibility. Obviously, some of my observations could and perhaps should be applied to other peoples of color or to whites. I will leave that project to another scholar or another time. This current reflection on black voice is a starting point, a significant one, I trust.

Perhaps the ulterior motive of this pursuit is more personal than scholarly. Like many other African Americans, I marvel at the number of whites and blacks who have told me that my voice either is "too black" or "not black enough." In most cases, when time and distance have allowed me to more objectively reflect on these accusations, I have not always been sure what my accusers mean. And if they are like most Americans when it comes to fathoming or articulating the complexities of race and voice, my accusers don't know what they mean either.

Acknowledgments

OF THE MANY SCHOLARS WHO HAVE INFLUENCED my thinking for this undertaking, W. Ross Winterowd and Keith Gilyard are at the forefront. Some of Winterowd's skepticism about rhetorical theories that rely too heavily on elusive metaphors has rubbed off on me, a former doctoral student of his. I have also adapted (decidedly beyond his original intent, I am sure) Ross's belief that scholarship in rhetoric and composition can maintain a useful dialogical relationship with literary scholarship, even when the major advocates from each of these respective camps would rather ignore the other.

I first became acquainted with Professor Gilyard in 1995 at the Conference on College Composition and Communication. I was and remain impressed with his uncanny facility to shift seamlessly from the academy vernacular to African American vernacular English. His verbal facility, it seems to me, transcends the technical descriptor "code switching." To be sure, Gilyard has the brains and boldness to interrogate the cultures from which these linguistic registers derive.

I especially thank Shirley Wilson Logan for her invaluable comments on early drafts of this manuscript. She opened my eyes to many historical and theoretical points that I had missed, although I am sure some ideological myopia remains.

Practically and personally speaking, this book could not have been completed were it not for the patient support of my wife, Veronica and my sons, Jonathan David and Gregory Matthew. Anything I have done or will do is richer because they are in my life.

Introduction

BY THE MID-NINETEENTH CENTURY, LITERACY WAS becoming codified
in terms of two highly charged concepts: "voice" and "race." This evolution can be traced in part by discussing the dilemma that Frederick
Douglass faces as he strives to mediate between the Romantic, or transcendental, voice Emerson posits and the public voice Caleb Bingham explicates in *The Columbian Orator*. Like other writers during the American Renaissance, Douglass oscillates between personal expression and
public communication as the ultimate purpose for writing.

During the 1850s, Douglass desires to be numbered with the "'I-narrators' of the American Renaissance" (Andrews, "*My*" 133). Yet Douglass's racial identity hinders his efforts. Douglass provides a minor case
study of how Romantic voice involves an enigma for people of color.
Hence I will not be critiquing Romantic voice directly but rather as it is
applied—through Douglass—to the practices and politics of literacy for
African Americans.

Nor am I contending that "voice" suggests exclusively thoughts of
Romanticism. On the contrary, it is a highly evocative term. A glance at
The Oxford English Dictionary reveals a wide range of meanings. *Voice*
covers an etymological terrain from the literal "phonology" to the metaphorical "conscience"; from a specific definition, such as "singing," to
a more overarching one, such as "sounds naturally made by a single per-

son or animal in speech or other forms of vocal utterance." This entry goes on for six pages and approximately three columns for each page.

Scholarly interpretations of metaphorical voice cover an even wider spectrum, from Walter Ong's affirmation that voice is presence to Jacques Derrida's denial of it as a part of his larger critique of Western logocentrism. For Derrida, literally or metaphorically, voice, scripting, and thinking are all types of writing.

When I use the word *voice,* I will be focusing on the interplay among the following definitions: (1) the Romantic sense of authorial presence, (2) a disenfranchised individual's or group's sociopolitical right to speak, and (3) literal voice, including standardized speech and aspects of the African American oral tradition.

The first definition of voice Emerson adopts from Plato. Frederick Douglass adopts the last two configurations of voice from *The Columbian Orator* as well as the discursive practices of the black church and slave culture. How these three definitions have been and can be used interchangeably, so that they mask assumptions regarding collective African American identity and ontology, constitute the basis for my reading of black voice in literature and composition.

Emerson's Romantic voice suggests a strategic place to introduce this study, therefore, not because he intended for his work to have implications for current debates about voice but because it does. This is the case whether one sees Emerson mainly as an idealistic sage or as a social critic. On the other hand, recognizing this duality may be precisely the point, for such a move constitutes one step in understanding Emerson's thought. F. O. Matthiessen opens his *American Renaissance* with a similar observation:

> The problem that confronts us in dealing with Emerson is the hardest we shall have to meet, because of his inveterate habit of stating things in opposites. The representative man whom he most revered was Plato. For Plato had been able to bridge the gap between the two poles of thought, to reconcile fact and abstraction, the many and the One, society and solitude. (3)

Matthiessen adds that Emerson could not easily achieve in his own thought the reconciliation that he revered in Plato's. Actually, Emerson characterizes his struggle to adapt Plato's philosophy to his own as "double consciousness." Emerson's neologism, which W. E. B. Du Bois would later appropriate to describe the existential trial informing the African American's experience in white America, marks the incessant tension between rational and metaphysical perception (Matthiessen 3–4).

The Platonic Influence on Emerson

Emerson's interest in Plato broaches the issue concerning which of Emerson's roles, philosopher or social critic, might be privileged over the other. This move becomes pertinent to this study, since the answers will be tailored to address voice in writing. Scholars as diverse as James Berlin, Ann E. Berthoff, Sharon Crowley, and Jasper Neel agree that Platonism is massively influential in composition theory. Since Emerson—one primary source of American values, philosophies, and attitudes—is a Platonist, tracing the Emersonian influence on composition becomes not only worthwhile but also necessary. Moreover, the tension in nineteenth-century African American literature between literal voice and written voice suggests an interesting twist on Plato's reading of Socrates.

In Plato's view, only through dialectic and live discourse can one hope to arrive at the truth, for writing is only a mnemonic technology, reminding us of what we already know. To be sure, through two of his dialogues, the *Phaedrus* and *Gorgias,* Plato uses his mentor, Socrates, and a group of stock characters to denigrate writing and rhetoric while exalting the pursuit of spiritual knowledge through dialectic. And although he despised writing, Plato would found inadvertently a writing tradition in which, as W. Ross Winterowd argues, inward contemplation and imagination would supplant invention. Emerson is an heir to that tradition.

As a result, the metaphor of written voice, or the contrast between authorial invention being primarily internal or external, emerges as an efficient way of comparing Plato and Emerson. After all, the debate over whether Emerson valorizes his role of introspective idealist over that of social critic hinges on such an exploration.

At the heart of Plato's legacy to Emerson, then, is this sense of doubling. The homage Emerson pays Plato in *Representative Men* presumably turns on Plato's ability to "transcend all sectional lines" (634). For Emerson, this transcendence typically manifests itself in the ways in which strains of Plato's philosophy inform divergent schools of thought: "Saxon" and "Roman," "Christianity" and "Mahometanism," to cite a couple of examples (633–34). According to Emerson, Plato was active in the intellectual, social, and political currents of his time, yet his "biography is interior" (635). To view Plato as merely a mystic with no interest in the pragmatic issues of his day, therefore, constitutes a gross misreading of both Emerson and Plato. Still, Plato elevates the esoteric over the pragmatic, viewing "all knowledge" as "anamnesis" or "based on previous experience of 'what the soul has learned'" (Segal x).[1]

A related instance of doubling arises in Emerson's essay on Plato in *Representative Men.* Emerson tries to create a small space where poetry and philosophy meet, and Plato occupies this space:

> A philosopher must be more than a philosopher. Plato is clothed with the powers of poet, stands upon the highest place of the poet, and (though I doubt he wanted the decisive gift of literary expression), mainly is not a poet because he chose to use the poetic gift to an ulterior purpose. (635)

To appreciate the significance of this passage, two facts should be kept in mind: the first encompasses the word *poetry,* the second, Plato's critique of poets. For ancient Greeks, poetry did not carry with it the specific connotations that had become popular by the Romantic period. The Greek word *poetikes,* from which *poetry* translates, means "to make" or "to imitate." Hence, all actions, including the kind presently ascribed to artistic performances (writing, painting, sculpting), are all manifestations of poetry. Perhaps in referring to Plato as a type of poet, Emerson acknowledges Plato's superlative talent for crafting thoughts that closely reflect ultimate ideas.

But why does Plato castigate the artistic poets in *The Republic,* for example? The answer can be found in the object of imitation. Artistic poets fail to fulfill Plato's lofty expectations because they imitate imitations, writing or painting about the natural world, whereas philosophers strive to arrive at essence, form, and the spiritual world. In fact, Plato denigrates writing particularly because it imitates speech, one step closer yet distinct from the spiritual realm. Emerson apparently understands both the etymology of the word *poetry* and Plato's disdain for artistic poets.

Even so, more than the preoccupation with the earthly instead of the celestial prompts Plato's critique of artistic poets. Plato believes artistic poets possess power to move the masses. In this way, they are much like rhetoricians. And as Plato (through Socrates) accuses rhetoricians of manipulating the masses in the *Gorgias,* so he levels the same charge against artistic poets in *The Republic.* Plato, then, dismantles the authority of artistic poets because they possess neither the knowledge to communicate spiritual realities nor the character if they did possess that knowledge.

This passage from *Representative Men* also exposes the clash in Emerson's thought between content and form. As Matthiessen points out, it is considerably difficult to establish a nexus between Emerson's "theory and practice" of "language and art" (4). Emerson spends most of his time focusing on content (Matthiessen 6), because such a move coincides with his "doctrine" that "asserts the superiority both of nature over art and of content over its vehicle" (Matthiessen 24). The writer or speaker must strive to unearth words that mirror the profundity of thought. What Emerson seeks, therefore, is "a form without boundaries." As a result, the medium to this limitless form is the potential "infinitude of the private man" (Matthiessen 6).

Emerson and Contemporary Composition

James Berlin and David S. Reynolds praise Emerson for his ardent participation in the public arena. Berlin contends that one can draw several parallels between Platonic and Emersonian epistemologies, the most notable being that "the ground of reality is the ideal." However, Emerson "departs from" Plato "as he locates the real in the fusion of the sensual and ideal" (*Writing* 46).

Berlin's aim in *Writing Instruction in Nineteenth-Century American Colleges* is to produce a standard history of composition in which he attempts to counter the allegation that Emerson is the source of neo-Romantic composition theory. For Berlin, the most common misreading of Plato's influence on Emerson stems from the assumption that they share congruous views of language, particularly about metaphor. Unlike Plato, Emerson believes that all men, not merely philosophers, can use metaphor. Berlin captures the point of this distinction when he notes,

> Without the language of the sensory, the ideal cannot be made manifest. Conversely, without the ideal, the world of nature is mere sense data without order or meaning. The point of intersection between outside and inside is language. (48)

For Berlin, this "intersection" redeems Emerson from the charge of being the progenitor of neo-Romantic composition. Rather, his rhetoric is demo-cratic, "everywhere dialectical—the result of the confrontation of idea and object, of speaker and event" (53).

Like Berlin, David S. Reynolds celebrates Emerson's role within the public domain but focuses on details regarding his sociopolitical activi-ties. He commends Emerson, for instance, for his objections to the treat-ment of the Cherokee Native Americans in 1838 and the Fugitive Slave Law of 1850 (93). More to the point, Emerson demonstrates his sympa-thy for the plight of oppressed people specifically and the common man generally through his rhetorical style, which he thought should be learned "in the street rather than the college" (94).

Still, Reynolds does not confuse Emerson's agenda with those of the other reformers of the nineteenth century. Emerson aspired to reform the reformers by balancing their "subversive reform spirit . . . with power-fully reconstructive philosophical elements," resulting in a "creative fusion" of "Conservatism and Reform" (95). Thus, resonating with Ber-lin and Matthiessen, Reynolds stresses Emerson's ability to reconcile opposing notions.

Notwithstanding the greatness of Emerson's participation within the public sphere, neither Berlin's nor Reynolds's arguments diminish the need for critiquing Emerson's Romantic legacy to writing theory and, by implication, pedagogy. Indeed, even Berlin's contention that Emerson's rhetoric is "preeminently concerned with the role of discourse in the public domain" begs several questions, the most pressing of which is this: how does Emerson cultivate this public discourse?

Certainly, as Reynolds opines, Emerson might have appropriated a few stylistic tips from the "common man in the street" for his lectures, but we might query, what is the heuristic that informs his content and arrangement, as well as the theory behind this heuristic? Or to frame the question more directly, you may use some of the common man's linguistic patterns, but *how* do you learn to speak to him?

Ironically, Berlin unintentionally implicates Emerson in the charge other composition scholars have leveled against him. The first line of the last paragraph of Berlin's chapter on Emerson in *Writing Instruction in Nineteenth-Century American Colleges* reads, "Emerson's rhetoric, not restricted to securing a desired effect on the audience, was attempting to restore the search for truth to the composing act" (57). This pronouncement suggests that despite Berlin's insistence that Emerson departed significantly from Plato in bridging the spiritual and physical realms, the "search for truth" places Emerson squarely and securely within the Platonic paradigm.

Constructed, tentative, or communal truth, which is not good enough for Plato or Emerson, is not only good enough for Aristotle but is also the more pragmatic rhetorical strategy. Hence, the *search for truth* approach to composing is flawed because *the* truth is neither accessible to the teacher nor, even if it were, teachable to the students.

Further, Berlin's qualifier "not restricted to securing a desired effect on the audience" should be scrutinized. Obviously, the rhetorical act of composing entails more than consideration of the audience. However, when applied to Emerson, such an observation also speaks to his elevation of the search for truth over the persuasion this search supposedly fosters. Consequently, the quest for truth becomes more virtuous than any moral pursuit or political conquest. Still further, the phrase trivializes the importance of invention or discovery in the composing act by almost deifying inspiration and creativity.[2] Writers retreat to the woods for the solitude and inspiration that will supposedly enable them to address the problems of the city.

Emerson's major enterprise forges a transcendental personal voice by which he could access the "One Mind" shared by other transcendentalists and potentially by all people.[3] His work reflects an oxymoron: the search for an inner public voice. Unfortunately, a large segment of his followers, writers who privilege inspiration over invention, are trapped by the very move (introspection) that supposedly liberates them. More to the point, these observations about Emerson, as we shall see shortly, have telling relevance for the evolution of Frederick Douglass's voice specifically and the codification of black voice generally.

1

The Color of Literacy:
Race, Self, and the Public Ethos

RALPH WALDO EMERSON EMPLOYED A ROMANTIC, or what I have called an "inner public," voice. Frederick Douglass was restricted by his efforts to appropriate a transracial public voice, despite his attempts to become an Emersonian "representative man." By the end of this chapter, I will have introduced how gender further complicated this restriction for women of color, like Frances E. W. Harper. Selected works of Douglass and Harper provide two sites for examining the nexuses among race, gender, and public voice. There are many other men and women of color one could consider in exploring the tensions between codified notions of race and literacy. However, Douglass and Harper will be more than adequate to illustrate my thesis.

To begin with, the titles of Frederick Douglass's three autobiographical narratives signify the evolution, or what Eric Sundquist calls "revisions," of his voice: *Narrative of the Life of Frederick Douglass, An American Slave; My Bondage and My Freedom;* and *The Life and Times of Frederick Douglass.* These titles indicate a progression from the slave narrative proper to American autobiography (Sundquist, *To Wake* 83–86). Douglass's prominence also illustrates how African American women were marginalized in the formation of African American letters, a practice that continued through the Black Arts movement.

Douglass's inability to transcend race raises several questions for this study, one of the most crucial being, who authenticates black voice? And here I am referring to political voice with implications for Romantic voice. For a period of several years, the white abolitionists with whom Douglass worked had to confirm the veracity of his voice as a black spokesperson representing other black slaves.

Not only did William Lloyd Garrison need to write a preface to the first edition of Douglass's narrative (a widespread convention for the publication of slave narratives), but also Douglass was told that his eloquence would eventually mar his credibility as a former slave. In other words, Douglass's narrative is among the first widely read literary vehicles to introduce the issues of colonization and ownership of black discourse. These issues are in currency today and often, as I hope to show by the end of this book, can hinder discussions about racialized identity and voice, even among African Americans themselves.

Definitions of black voice particularly, then, involve far too many vistas for this chapter to adequately address. Therefore I must construct a manageable entrance into the subject. Douglass and Harper will provide me with that entrance. Indeed, *construct* will be one of the operative words of my analysis, as it should be for this or any other study that seeks to flesh out and juxtapose elusive notions like race and voice.

Both Emerson and Douglass are primarily reformers. In fact, Eric Sundquist places Douglass within a major tradition of African American protest, one that rather than dismantling the current system, strives to revise it *(To Wake)*.[1] While some of Douglass's contemporaries, Martin Delany for example, argued for what became Black Nationalism, Douglass opted for full integration (if at times tempered by slow economic advancement) into the American mainstream. Consequently, Douglass eventually dissented with abolitionists, like his mentor Garrison, who desired to abrogate the Declaration of Independence and the Constitution for dehumanizing African Americans.

For Douglass and Emerson, reform requires more than change as an end in itself. Reform involves redrawing ideological and social boundaries. Emerson does this mostly through theoretical musings, while Douglass, more practically, broadens the purview of America's founding documents to include her citizens of color. Both enterprises converge at the points of identity and voice: who is to be heard, how, and why?

In terms of the media employed to redefine these boundaries, Douglass and Emerson foreground their respective reforms in the interplay between orality and literacy. They both enjoyed wide acclaim for their twofold reputation as lecturers and writers, their paths crossing a few times while engaged in these roles. For instance, Emerson contributed a poem and Douglass his novella, *The Heroic Slave,* to *Autographs of Freedom,* a gift book of antislavery writings published in 1853. Edited by British abolitionist Julia Griffiths, the book was sold to raise money for Douglass's "financially troubled" *North Star* (Sundquist, *To Wake* 115).

One vital way to distinguish Emerson's ethos from Douglass's, however, is to examine the extent to which the private self controls or is controlled by the audience reception of the public self. For Douglass, writing and lecturing are more than media of self-expression; orality and literacy correspondingly function as vehicles for self-definition and self-preservation. Douglass's demonstration of literacy and resolve to be courageous led to his psychological liberation. He could only be a "slave in form" while "not in fact" (*Narrative* 299). On the other hand, because white society chose Douglass as spokesperson for his race, the collective ethos of all other African Americans would largely obfuscate his individual ethos.

Before introducing how America's race ideology thwarted Douglass's intention to formulate a transracial public voice, I will review one major source of his public voice, Bingham's *The Columbian Orator.* In chapter 7 of the *Narrative,* Douglass recounts his initial encounter with Bingham's book, intimating that it was pivotal to his intellectual coming-of-age:

> I was now about twelve years old, and the thought of being a
> slave for life began to bear heavily upon my heart. Just about
> this time, I got a hold of a book entitled "The Columbian Ora-
> tor." Every opportunity I got, I used to read this book. Among
> much of the interesting matter, I found in it a dialogue between
> a master and his slave. The slave was represented as having
> run away from his master three times. The dialogue repre-
> sented the conversation which took place between them, when
> the slave was retaken the third time. In this dialogue, the whole
> argument in behalf of slavery was brought forward by the
> master, all of which was disposed of by the slave. The slave

> was made to say some very smart as well as impressive things
> in reply to his master—things which had the desired though
> unexpected effect: for the conversation resulted in the volun-
> tary emancipation of the slave on the part of the master. (278)

To describe the above passage as recounting Douglass's intellectual coming-of-age coincides with the purpose and scope of *The Columbian
Orator*. Authored by Caleb Bingham, the book was a speech primer
"committed to the proposition that American boys, as the inheritors of
a tradition of oratory, were destined to speak the virtues of a new republic" (McFeely 34). Indeed, oratory is, as inscribed on the book's title
page, both "ornamental" and "useful."

Originally published in 1797, Bingham's book was unquestionably
popular, being republished twenty-three times and selling two hundred
thousand copies in fifty years. The introduction, providing "General
Instructions for Speaking" (2–29), focuses on pronunciation, gestures,
and practical rules for using gestures and voice. Pronunciation is the
"principal part of the orator's province," or so confirm classical rhetors
like Cicero and Demosthenes, and the "more natural pronunciation is,
the more moving" (Bingham 10).

Similarly, the orator's "gestures and countenance" should harmonize
with subject matter. One should never, for instance, "wring hands, tear
hair, or strike the breast," unless one wishes to strongly indicate sorrow
(Bingham 10). While Bingham encourages speakers to use a higher-pitch
voice when narrating, "matters of fact should be retold in a very plain
and distinct manner" (25).

The bulk of Bingham's text contains model speeches. Notably, these
speeches cover a wide range of periods, genres, and subjects. Chrono-
logically, the settings of these discourses shift from ancient Rome to eighteenth-century England and America. There are speeches given to Par-
liament and Congress, sermons, student exhibitions, and dialogues.
Whether legal, political, ceremonial, or personal discourse, each model
is rigidly structured and, hence, easily imitated. "The Dialogue Between
an English Duellist, a North American Savage and Mercury" (Bingham
50–54), for instance, enacts a conversation among three ghosts. While
clearly fictitious, the piece purports to detail for the readers how to con-
duct a dialogue after death.

In the same way, the address "Lines Spoken by a Little Boy," ideally written by the boy himself for a school exhibition, is vintage neoclassical oratory, framed in heroic couplets and containing allusions to Cicero and Caesar. The underlying message becomes clear: if your son studies this speech, he can produce the same quality of oratory.

For the pubescent Douglass, the hard-earned purchase and dogged appropriation of the Bingham text was his first step into America's intellectual commonplace. Later during his career, Douglass would draw on other sources for his speeches and writings: the public lectures of William H. Channing, Henry Giles, Wendell Phillips, Daniel Webster, and Emerson, whom Douglass considered "America's literary patriarch." As "an avid reader," Douglass also made use of the Bible, Shakespeare, Longfellow, Dickens, and Dumas, as well as pamphlets and newspapers.[2] But it was *The Columbian Orator,* probably the only standard guide to oratory Douglass used (Blassingame xxii), that in theory placed him in the same position as his white counterparts to appreciate the magnificent "tradition of oratory."

That Douglass confronted the obstacles that racism imposed upon him, however, may attest to a profounder appreciation for the import of Bingham's text than his free, white peers may have possessed. Douglass's biographer, William McFeely, affirms Douglass's conversion to the proposition Bingham articulates in his introduction: namely, that speech can conquer the hearts of soldiers. "Caesar . . . upon hearing Cicero speak, fell into a fit of 'shivering'" (McFeely 34). The rhetorically well-spoken word was empowering.

Yet the power of the spoken word was not the principal attribute that drew Douglass to Bingham's book. Douglass was mostly taken by its uncompromising denunciation of American slavery (McFeely 35). This denunciation confirmed his increasing faith in the natural equality of all men. Consequently, the text proclaimed universal liberty in theory, even if most of the whites that read its pages failed to apply this theory to the slave's plight.

Furthermore, much of the power of *The Columbian Orator* comes from the stress given to the interdependence between speaker and audience, a strategy that Shelley Fisher Fishkin and Carla L. Peterson style as "dialogic" in a Bakhtinian sense (191). Fishkin and Peterson are evidently alluding to Mikhail Bakhtin's neologism *heteroglossia,*[3] which suggests that original or individual utterances do not actually exist. Rather, speakers' utterances are a part of a network of the past and present utterances of others, including the audiences to whom they speak. All so-called individual utterances are, therefore, "multivocal."

I do not fully embrace Fishkin and Peterson's claim that "techniques of the dialogic" are "the most prominent oratorical devices" employed throughout *The Columbian Orator*. It is worthwhile, nonetheless, to consider their essay when referring to "The Dialogue Between a Master and Slave." On the surface, this selection does appear dialogic, especially since it qualifies as a Socratic dialogue. After a prologue summarizing the injustice of slavery, the eloquent slave poses a series of inductive questions that lead his master to an inescapable denial of his right to continue to enslave another human being. The interchange, characteristic of query and response, supposedly highlights the speaker's regard for his audience.

However, comparable to the Socratic method, "The Dialogue Between a Master and Slave" is really not audience-centered at all but subversively speaker-centered. Granted, this fact should not necessarily invite skepticism, given the persuasive intent of both Bingham and Socrates. Still, this dialogue leaves little room for anything other than a stock consideration of audience. Contrary to Douglass's belief, the end of this dialogue is certainly predictable.

Ironically, however, the African American call-and-response tradition may prove to be more dialogic and, thereby, more cooperative than the aforementioned strategy. The relatively free and improvised structure of call and response affords speaker and audience with a variety of communicative options. Therefore I do not intend for my focus on *The Columbian Orator* to trivialize the influence of the African American Church on Douglass's oratory. In fact, as Jacqueline Bacon and Glen McClish have observed, black orators often adapted standardized treatises on oratory, like Hugh Blair's *Lectures on Belles Lettres,* for their own addresses. Obviously, black preachers could have made a similar move with *The Columbian Orator.*

In fact, Gregory P. Lampe's study, *Frederick Douglass: Freedom's Voice, 1818–1845,* traces the extensive influence of the black oral tradition on the evolution of Douglass's oratory. Lampe carries his readers from Douglass's childhood of listening to folktales, songs, and sermons to his conducting a Sabbath school class as a young adult slave, to his serving as a "licensed lay preacher" well into his days of abolitionist fame. Even so, *The Columbian Orator* represents one of the few modes of literacy that the racist America of his time would accept: so-called standardized literacy.

While *The Columbian Orator,* then, empowers Douglass to construct a public voice, it alone would delimit his rhetorical alternatives, partly because of the confined structure of "The Dialogue Between a Master and Slave," yet largely because of the regularizing of style the entire text of *The Columbian Orator* fosters. Just as Emerson's Romantic voice attempts to universalize the internal, the public voice of *The Columbian Orator* aims to regularize orality, to conventionalize even the more informal speech acts, such as an informal argument between two people.

Moreover, as transcendentalism demarcates the tension between idealism and social critique, the ornamentation engendered by Bingham's public voice acutely influences the shape moral discourse obtains. Echoing the assumptions of what Winterowd calls the "methodism" of the eighteenth century, *The Columbian Orator* contributes to the standardization of belles lettres during the nineteenth century. Juxtaposing the private, metaphorical voice of Emerson with the public, literal voice of *The Columbian Orator,* therefore, mirrors the Romantic desire to correlate introspection with expression. As a result of this juxtaposition, however, the public voice adopts the metaphorical station associated with the internal, Romantic voice.

What hinders Douglass from realizing a transracial public voice? In a phrase, one legacy of the Enlightenment: racial essence, more specifically, the assumed inherent, intellectual inferiority of the African. By the nineteenth century, a triad linking race and language, with being at the apex, was definitely taking form. And Douglass's failed attempt to transcend race in the projection of his public persona verifies this. Douglass's failure, however, cannot be attributed to his lack of motivation or effort.

His steps toward literacy, including adoption of *The Columbian Orator,* were met with other moments of psychological epiphany. From his former master's acerbic objection to his wife teaching the boy Douglass the rudiments of reading—"Learning would spoil the best nigger. . . . It would make him unfit to be a slave" (Douglass, *Narrative* 274)—to the slightly older Douglass, who would trade the appeasement of physical hunger for the self-actualization to be realized with the bread of knowledge, Douglass longed for the empowerment and total liberty literacy promised.

But this promise was not fulfilled. From his lectures for the New England abolitionists to the publication of the first installment of his narrative in 1845, on to the establishment of his own newspaper, the *North Star,* and other independent excursions in orality and literacy, Douglass's efforts to create a transracial voice met with formidable resistance. This resistance was rooted in the paradigm of race. Or as Wilson J. Moses opines, "His development as an artist and intellectual was circumscribed by the time and place in which he was born" (66). This circumscribing is manifested in the "tactful confinement" of the slave narrative and the insistence on the part of the white abolitionists that Douglass lecture using "the plantation vernacular." Also, Douglass demonstrated an inability to "completely abandon the slave narrative formula in any version of his autobiography," though "he struggled increasingly to escape its confines" (Moses 67).

One of the signs of Douglass's time, which would increasingly surface in the successive versions of his autobiography, was the public projection of himself as a representative, American man: "Like Emerson, Lincoln, and Barnum, he interpreted his life as a moral precept, inviting his contemporaries to learn from his experiences and to weave them into the developing web of American values" (Moses 69).

African American physician and abolitionist James McCune Smith concurs. Writing the introduction to Douglass's second major revision of his narrative *My Bondage and My Freedom,* Smith lauds Douglass as "A Representative American Man—a type of his countrymen" (qtd. in Andrews, "My" 133). Concerning the significance of "Representative Men," William L. Andrews says,

> In speaking of Douglass as representative, Smith asked his readers to think of this quality in a distinctly Emersonian sense, as denoting a kind of epitome or standard by which others might measure themselves. To Emerson, "representative men" served as examples *to,* not of, the general run of humankind because such men revealed "moral truths" to "the general mind." (134)

One compelling reason, therefore, why Douglass failed to construct a transracial public voice is that "his enslavement is a part of *his* American success story." However, prior to Douglass, and later Booker T. Washington, few if any whites associated slavery with an *American* experience; rather, it was a uniquely southern black experience.

To be sure, neither Emerson's transcendental contemplation nor Douglass's public literacy could empower one to completely transcend the American race paradigm. Furthermore, the public voice of *The Columbian Orator* and the introspective voice of Romanticism isolate the dichotomy between the conventional and the ideal, the external and the internal. Douglass stages his awareness of this dichotomy in his only work of fiction, *The Heroic Slave*. Written in 1853, this reenactment of an actual slave insurrection curiously subverts and reifies codified notions of public voice. The novella opens with Douglass ascribing to his protagonist the virtues of a Virginia statesman:

> The state of Virginia is famous in American annals for the multitudinous array of her statesmen and heroes. She has been dignified by some as the mother of statesmen. . . . By some strange neglect, one of the truest, manliest, and bravest of her children—one who, in after years, will, I think, command the pen of genius to set his merits forth, holds now no higher place in the records of that grand old Commonwealth than is held by a horse or an ox. ("The Heroic Slave" 25)

Douglass arouses the empathy of his readers (presumably patriotic and white) for the protagonist. He will further accentuate this empathy by comparing the protagonist's love for and right to liberty with Patrick Henry and Thomas Jefferson respectively. Both moves evince Douglass's rhetorical acumen, for not until the third page does he reveal that the protagonist, Madison Washington (note the name), is a slave. Douglass wishes to convince his readers that his protagonist has not only the abstract qualities of an American hero and statesman but the physical bearing as well:

> Madison was of manly form. Tall, symmetrical, round, and strong. In his movements he seemed to combine, with the strength of the lion, a lion's elasticity. His torn sleeves disclosed

arms like polished iron. His face was "black, but comely." His eye, lit with emotion, kept guard under a brow as dark and as glossy as the raven's wing; yet there was nothing savage or forbidding in his aspect. ("Heroic" 28)

By coupling abstract qualities with physical appearance, Douglass hopes to dismantle the most insidious form of nineteenth-century racism, as well as establish Washington's public ethos. By positing a definitive nexus between Washington's cultivated virtues and his biologically determined physical appearance, Douglass inverts the paradigm of racism used against people of color and thereby dismantles its authority. In the same manner, Douglass conflates the monstrous character of the slave traders with demonic countenance:

By this time the keepers arrived. A horrid trio, well fitted for demoniacal work. Their uncombed hair came down over their foreheads "villainously low," and with eyes, mouths, and noses to match. "Hallo!" "hallo!" they growled out as they entered. ("Heroic" 55)

With the exception of three other white characters, those promoting slavery are depicted as barbaric and profoundly stupid. Wilkes, a named representative of the Virginia tavern dwellers, drivels and rambles in a language far more incomprehensible than anyone could assume slave dialect to be. Similarly, the sailors aboard the *Creole* slave ship are portrayed as "frightened monkeys" and "black cats."

One wonders, however, what Douglass sacrifices in his enterprise with this admittedly shrewd strategy of racialized inversion. To begin with, in sundry ways Douglass reminds his readers of Listwell's judgment of Washington: he is guilty of "no crime save the color of his skin." Impressed with Washington's intelligence, courage, and sincerity, the first mate of the *Creole*, Tom Grant, would have followed Washington during the insurrection he led, "had he been a white man" (68).

Nevertheless, for a book that seemingly invests so much in color, or better yet, discrimination against the protagonist based on his blackness, Washington is ostensibly colorless. The description of Washington detailed above could easily serve as a prototype for any European hero in the Western tradition. Granted, Douglass concedes Washington's blackness, but by qualifying this trait with "comely," he anticipates and quickly diffuses any fears his audience might have of black "savages." Moreover, by spending virtually no time telling his readers more precisely what he means by "black" as a physical trait, Douglass may be unintentionally deprecating the people he longs to honor.

In appropriating what Richard Yarborough calls America's "white bourgeois paradigm of manhood," Douglass may be inadvertently sabotaging his own project, since "his celebration of black heroism was subverted from the outset by the racist, sexist, and elitist assumptions upon which the Anglo-American male ideal was constructed" (Yarborough 182).

The explication of Washington's literal voice also becomes questionable. Parenthetically, Douglass styles this voice "that unfailing index of the soul" ("Heroic" 28). In doing so, Douglass recalls a kind of Platonic valorizing of Washington's voice particularly and orality generally. Apparently, he uses Washington to illuminate what Douglass learned from *The Columbian Orator:* the well-spoken word is power. In contrast to Douglass, however, the readers of "The Heroic Slave" are not privy to Washington's literate source of oratorical prowess.

Obviously Washington was, as Douglass, self-educated. Yet the exclusion of the process by which his learning occurs constitutes the novella's central enigma. Tom Grant's appraisal of Washington in the novella, after the protagonist's mutiny aboard the *Creole,* suggests a comparable judgment:

> He seldom spake to any one, and when he did speak, it was with the utmost propriety. His words were well chosen, and his pronunciation equal to that of any schoolmaster. It was a mystery to us *where* he got his knowledge of language; but as little was said to him, none of us knew the extent of his intelligence and ability until it was too late. (65)

As a point of fact, the "where" appears to be a Virginia forest, and this fact presents a quandary. During the story's opening scene, Washington's soon to be ally, Listwell, travels by the forest in question. While doing so, Listwell overhears Washington, who is musing aloud, planning his escape from slavery. These musings unfold into a harangue reminiscent of a Shakespearean soliloquy, the opening query—"What, then, is life to me?"—recalling Hamlet's "To be or not to be?" Nevertheless, one essential rhetorical element (pathos) is trivialized, while Romantic voice and ornament are elevated.

The central issue is not Washington's orality and literacy but rather how he cultivates these skills; one viable option readers are left with is the Emersonian contemplation of nature. In like manner, however, one should not assume that Emerson totally dismisses rhetorical invention simply because he privileges retreating to and reflecting upon nature. Still, this privileging is crucial. One brief passage from "Nature" should clarify this point: "To go into solitude, a man needs to retire as much from his chamber as from society. I am not solitary whilst I read and write though nobody is with me. But if a man would be alone, let him look at the stars" (74). This solitude fosters the kind of "insight" one indirectly receives via tradition and religion ("Nature" 73). Neither solitude (especially in the case of a slave like Washington, for whom the forest becomes more a place of refuge than contemplation) nor critically questioning great minds represents the central dilemma. Rather, what is to be done prior to, during, and after these moments of solitude in order to communicate with others?

Similarly, the fact that Listwell secretly overhears Washington's soliloquy begs a larger question: how central is the presence of Listwell or any listener to constructing Washington's public ethos? That Washington's private speech moves Listwell to liken him to a "sable preacher" of "rare endowments" further complicates the question, especially since preaching (particularly black preaching with its highly interactive process known as "call and response") fully relies on considerations of audience for both the preparation and delivery of sermons.

If literate discourse had attained by the Enlightenment the level of importance Gates ascribes to it and if the nineteenth century represents a more concentrated effort on the part of African Americans "to write themselves into humanity," Douglass's portrayal of Madison Washington is most peculiar. The only evidence of written literacy is found in a brief letter Washington scrawls to Listwell ("Heroic" 46).

Thus Douglass's effort to mediate between the transcendental voice of Romanticism and the public voice of *The Columbian Orator* was thwarted by an evolving race ideology. By the nineteenth century, many white Americans had already begun linking literacy with race and ontology, thus forming a paradigm that, for the African American, could be transcended neither by introspection nor in the projection of articulate public discourse.

Harper and the Racialized Sexism of Public Discourse

Frances E. W. Harper exemplifies the many women of color during the nineteenth century who had to construct an effective rhetorical ethos despite not only racism but sexism as well. Shirley Wilson Logan has shown that Harper falls within a tradition of African American women rhetors, Maria Stewart and Ida B. Wells-Barnett among them, who employed variegated strategies to persuade different audiences and readers, including men and women, blacks and whites. Accordingly, Logan suggests that Harper's contribution was a part of larger efforts African American women orators made toward improving their political, social, and religious status through "church, clubs, and societies."

Because of the rub of gender, therefore, Harper's life was characterized by more ambiguities than was Douglass's, even though there are some clear similarities between them. She was born free in the slave state from which Douglass escaped. Similar to Douglass, she experienced, as an orphan, the psychological isolation of not knowing all of her relatives. She developed early her love for the written and spoken word; however, Harper was trained formally at the William Watkins Academy for Negro Youth. Located in Baltimore, the school specialized in the classical curriculum encompassing the Bible, elocution, and languages.

Like Douglass's, Harper's construction of voice covered a variety of mediums, although she was the more prolific writer. Primarily a journalist, Harper was also an essayist, poet, novelist, and short story writer. By 1854, Harper was a full-time antislavery lecturer. Her writings and oratory would critique a range of human indignities, including racism, sexism, and classism.

In a real sense, Harper's and Douglass's respective uses of fiction, as well as those of some of the other writers I will consider in subsequent chapters, were polemical. Although ornately crafted, their fiction does not focus on art for art's sake. Granted, polemical fiction can be restricted neither to the antebellum period nor to black authors. Harper and other African American authors, however, write with a rhetorical intent that does not allow for the wholesale endorsement of genre distinctions. Indeed, these writers suggest an ideology of genres that foreshadows and inverts Winterowd's thesis in *The Rhetoric of the "Other" Literature*. In this book, Winterowd argues that if we can come to appreciate non-literary texts (essays, biographies, historical treatises, travelogues, and even utility texts) for artistic reasons, then the distinction between fiction and nonfiction becomes, to some degree, arbitrary. Likewise, Harper would not cling to any concrete distinctions between her fiction and nonfiction that would obfuscate her larger persuasive purposes.

Not surprisingly, Harper's last major work of fiction, *Iola Leroy,* manifests clearly this persuasive intent. But more important, the novel crystallizes Harper's convictions against racism, classism, and sexism. Originally published in 1892, *Iola Leroy* was the most widely read African American novel of the time and was reprinted five times during its first years of publication.

Harper sets the novel at the end of the Civil War, and the Union Army had already occupied a wooded area near the unnamed town in North Carolina where Iola Leroy is a slave. After the narrative progresses with the story of a few male slaves who plan on escaping to join the Union forces, the protagonist is introduced in chapter 5. In concert with the sentimental formula for nineteenth-century novels about white women, her initial description strikes a balance among beauty, virtue, and courage. Tom Anderson, the slave who aids Iola in her escape to the Union camp, describes her as lovely woman with blue eyes, long hair, and skin "jis ez white ez anybody's in dis place" (31). Yet she was not only "beautiful but intractable," resisting formidably the advances of a master "who had tried in vain to drag her down to his own low level of sin and shame."

Iola's life illustrates the level of pathos that Harper sought in her speeches and essays. Iola was the daughter of a white Mississippi planter, Eugene Leroy, and a mother, Marie, who was a quadroon and her father's former slave. After falling in love with the ostensibly white Marie, Eugene emancipates her, sends her to the north to be educated and eventually marries her. Choosing to carefully guard Maria's racial origins from their children, Iola and her two siblings grow up believing that they are white and that slavery can be benevolent, a behavior her father supposedly modeled. Iola adamantly defends the potential humanity of slavery, as she debates with her classmates in the northern university she attends. But Iola's moral conversion occurs under tragic circumstances.

While preparing to graduate, her father dies of yellow fever, and his racist cousin finds a way to render the Leroys' marriage void. Marie is enslaved, and soon after her return to Mississippi, so is Iola.

When she uncovers the truth about her background, Iola begins to evolve into a much stronger opponent of slavery than she had been a proponent. To be sure, she develops an ethos that resonates with the one Harper projects in her writings and speeches. Not only does Iola reject the racial status her complexion would have afforded her had she chosen to pass for white, but she also walks away from the social comfort of marriage by rejecting the proposal of the white Union Army doctor, Gresham. Her choices are more than existential, for Iola has a keen interest in the plight of suffering people. As a result, she becomes a teacher for the newly freed slaves and later an activist for blacks and women.

Like Douglass but more than her principal character, Iola Leroy, Harper achieved such an astounding level of identification with her audiences through language that many of them wanted to dissociate her from her identity markers. Hazel Carby notes that "some audiences thought Harper [Watkins's later married name] must be a man, while others thought she couldn't possibly be black and had to be painted" (rpt. in Foner and Branham 304). More than demonstrating the racism and sexism coded into so-called "standardized" usage of language during the nineteenth century, Carby's remarks speak to Harper's ability to employ language to function as an *honorary* insider.

Harper's convictions against injustice, however, would not allow her to remain an insider for long. She could at once identify with an audience for the common struggle they shared yet challenge that same audience for not being more concerned about a struggle that they did not share. She enacts one classic example of this strategy in her speech "We Are All Bound Up Together." Delivered in 1866 at the Eleventh National Women's Rights Convention in New York, the speech places Harper, as Shirley Wilson Logan has observed, in the dual roles of insider and outsider. She begins her address by alluding to the wrongs she has suffered because of her race and places these wrongs within a larger context of sufferings that are not just racial in origin. Foreshadowing Martin Luther King's claim that all people are "wrapped in a garment of destiny," Harper opines, "We are all bound together in one great bundle of humanity, and society cannot trample one of its feeblest members without receiving the curse of its own soul." She levels this "curse" against rich slaveholders whose nefarious socioeconomic practices dehumanized blacks and marginalized poor white men. The climax of the first half of the speech occurs when Harper argues that the current social revolution will not be successful until the "American Republic" looks beyond race, class, and gender.

Harper opens the second part of her speech with a remark that delineates the difference between her social perspective and that of her audience:

> You white women here speak of rights. I speak of wrongs. I, as a colored woman, have had an education which has made me feel as if I were in the situation of Ishmael, my hand against every man, and every man's hand against me. Let me go tomorrow morning to take my seat in one of your street cars— I do not know that they will do it in New York, but they will in Philadelphia—and the conductor will put up his hand and stop the car rather than let me ride. ("We" 459)

More telling than Harper's shift of emphasis in subject matter is her broadening of the geographical borders of discrimination, a proposition that many of her audience were unwilling to accept. For Harper, discrimination is a northern as well as southern problem. One audience member interrupted Harper's speech at this point to assure her that segregation on streetcars did not occur in New York, a tacitly guilty response to be sure. Nevertheless, Harper establishes a geographical and sociological divide between her and her audience. Like Ishmael from the Old Testament, blacks may be related to Abraham, the father of prosperity (and by implication Abraham Lincoln), but they were not sharing in that prosperity the way their white brother Isaac was.

However, Harper does not articulate this divide to be divisive. Instead, the distinctions that she underscores are meant to persuade her white listeners to be more active in empowering blacks by exposing what Cornel West calls the "multi-contextual" dimensions of identity. On some levels, Harper, and all people for that matter, could share common ground, while on other matters they would not. Shirley Wilson Logan describes the same issue of the black woman rhetor's mediation between insider and outsider as "convergence" and "divergence" (Logan, ch. 3).

The particular theme of people of color remaining outsiders even while mastering the standardized language of the insiders has been explored in more contemporary autobiographical excursions. Keith Gilyard's *Voices of the Self* and bell hooks's "'When I Was a Young Soldier for the Revolution': Coming to Voice" remain worthy of consideration.

Hence, Frederick Douglass's belief in the transracial reality of public voice was as futile for the person of color as was Emerson's trust in the transcending value of Romantic voice and Harper's demonstration of transgendered and transracial rhetorical competence. All three underestimated the pervasive power of the subtext of race. In other words, so-called colorless public literacy, transgendered oratory, and transcendental contemplation reflected a racialized image.

2

From Reading Race to Race as a Way of Reading

BLACK VOICE IS A SLIPPERY METAPHOR PARTLY because its two operative terms *(race* and *voice)* are elusive and culturally charged. Indeed, all literal and many figurative ways of describing race in America have been flawed because race remained an object to be interpreted or read rather than a way of reading culture. From the late nineteenth to early twentieth century, these flawed views evolved into codified interconnections among race, language, and being that have informed the appropriation of voice as a shibboleth in the history of African American writing.

Notwithstanding the voluminous work that has been done on critical race studies, rhetoric composition scholars must continue to interrogate the historical import of race and writing. If an ever-broadening knowledge of the sociopolitical histories of ancient Greece and Rome are requisite for applying classical rhetoric to contemporary writing instruction, even more relevant are ongoing explorations of American race histories in constructing increasingly more mobile paradigms for black voice in composition studies. Ongoing historical excursions might encourage composition scholars to replace literal and figurative readings of race (such as Henry Louis Gates's metaphors "race as text and trope") with, among other constructions, the notion of "race as a cultural hermeneutic."[1] Neither the notion of race as a way of reading nor the phrase "race as hermeneutic" is entirely new. Nevertheless, many theoretical and pedagogical implications remain unexplored as this notion and phrase inform rhetoric composition studies.

Racist Doctrines

Any historical survey of black voice, therefore, should start with the more fundamental question of what has constituted "blackness." From the 1870s to the 1920s, biological and linguistic boundaries of blackness, arbitrary within themselves, had come to demarcate the more arbitrary boundaries of psychological and spiritual blackness. The oldest and most common indicators of biological blackness (those predating the nineteenth century) were the visible differences between Africans and Europeans: primarily complexion but also hair, nose, and lips. Later, complexion came to be construed as the cultural or, in more cases, genetic sign of inferiority—that is, a sign of difference ironically more than skin deep.

Scientific and philosophical rationales influenced by religious ideology during all of the eighteenth century had become, by the middle of the nineteenth century, divorced from this ideology. One way to chart the complete transition from the less religious to the more secular construction of blackness, therefore, is to understand the difference between what Thomas Gossett has called the "monogenetic" and "polygenetic" theories of race origins.

In the main, eighteenth-century thinkers embraced the former theory, which claimed that all people (regardless of race) were a part of the same species. Hence, "all men" (the sexist exclusiveness of this phrase and the period notwithstanding) were originally created "equal." This theory alludes to the Old Testament but primarily comes from John Locke's natural rights philosophy and Thomas Jefferson's adaptation of the Magna Carta.[2]

The first forty years of the nineteenth century chronicled a shift from the monogenetic and religious theory of race origins toward the polygenetic and secular theory.[3] The polygenists believed that separate races evinced distinct species. A number of scholars and scientific journals clung to this theory until 1859, the year Charles Darwin's *Origin of the Species* appeared. Samuel George Morton, George Robin Gliddon, and Josiah Clark Nott were the most distinguished advocates of polygeneticism. They predictably enjoyed attacking the fundamentalist Christian stance on creation (Gossett 64; Stanton 162).

Morton was the "most eminent scientific member" of the Academy of Natural Sciences of Philadelphia (Stanton 1). Amid "the confused speculation about the origin of the races," his *Crania Americana*, published in 1839, "was hailed as a solution to the whole problem" (25). A physician and anatomy professor, Morton was best known as a craniologist. He was among the first to measure the skulls of various races, concluding that Caucasians had the largest skulls and, as a result, the largest brains and the greatest capacity for thought (32). Conversely, the Ethiopians had the smallest skulls and, therefore, brains.

Since Morton's research led him to conclude that people could be divided into "twenty-two families," he discredited Thomas Jefferson's environmental hypothesis. Curiously, as Stanton notes, Morton avoids using the word *species,* preferring *families* (33). Doing so, despite his allegiance to Archbishop James Usher's chronology of the Genesis flood, indicates that Morton was assertive in his break from the religious traditions associated with monogeneticism, yet not quite as bold as his protégés Gliddon and Nott would be.

An English businessman and amateur Egyptologist, Gliddon eventually persuaded Morton to discard Usher's chronology (Stanton 50). Regarding Gliddon and Nott's eight-hundred-page treatise *Types of Mankind,* Thomas Gossett concludes, "From the standpoint of science, it was important mainly because it collected a great deal of Morton's work; but it also spread the polygenist idea of the origin of the races to a wider and more popular reading public" (Gossett 65). As a result, what we would now call "pseudoscientific" views of race became popular. And although Darwin's *Origin of the Species* ironically discredited both the polygenist and monogenist theories (Gossett 66–68), America still found intellectualized justification for humiliating her people of color.

It is not surprising that Frederick Douglass opposed Gliddon and Nott's book, which contained bigoted declarations such as "nonwhite races are incapable of taking the first step towards civilization . . . unless" the individual in question "had at least one white ancestor" (Gossett 65). Douglass based his repudiation of *Types of Mankind* on two premises, the first being the authors' political aspirations, the second his own contention that "ancient Egyptians had a generous admixture of Negro blood" (66). Douglass's first premise was ignored and his second dismissed, since he "could find few students of Egyptology who agreed with him" (66). As a result, Douglass's eloquent speeches and writings, in which he argued for an America free enough to respect people of color as fellow citizens, were like shouts to the wind.

Black Dialect and Black Ontology

But America's flawed definition of blackness was based on more than phenotypic features like complexion. Many also believed dialect to be a way of measuring black identity. This is not to say that language and Romantic voice are synonymous. Internal voice or authorial presence is elusive and abstract, whereas African American vernacular English (AAVE), as one manifestation of language, is concrete and measurable. One cannot speak intelligently, however, about the evolution of black voice (in the private or public sense) without exploring the influence of AAVE. While whites from the eighteenth to the early twentieth century were claiming a natural union between the physical appearance of blacks and their moral and intellectual ineptitude, the same assumptions were being made on the basis of dialect.

As J. L. Dillard has observed, the "thick lips" theory, which supposedly explained why blacks spoke dialect, had become popular by the nineteenth century. In contrast, H. L. Mencken, in *The American Language* (1919), and Richard Walser, in his "Negro Dialect in Eighteenth Century Drama" (1955), were among many whites who questioned the origin of AAVE. Whereas Mencken could not decide "whether he was dealing with something real or something invented by literary men," Walser "suggested that playwrights *created* dialect" (Dillard 7). Of course the artists of whom Mencken and Walser spoke were white.

One might expect, then, that within the artistic arena, assumptions about dialect, identity, and essence made the most significant strides. The plantation fiction of Joel Chandler Harris and Thomas Nelson Page entertained white readers with the "authentic" representation of black dialect. In the same manner, minstrel shows, invented by whites during the nineteenth century, supposedly afforded white audiences with a window into the collective soul of black people.[4]

That white artists adopted AAVE for their work troubled some African American writers. In the preface to the 1921 edition of *The Book of American Negro Poetry,* James Weldon Johnson criticized white writers for restricting their use of dialect to orthographic distortions.[5] Further, white writers, according to Johnson, limited the emotional and topical spectrum of vernacular within their narratives (Jones 12). Because of these misuses, Johnson predicted that black writers would avoid employing dialect the way white writers had in their fiction.[6] Ten years later, in the preface to another edition of the same anthology, Johnson would alter his stance on dialect, since younger African American writers, such as Langston Hughes, Zora Neale Hurston, and Sterling Brown were expanding artistic approaches beyond Johnson's syntactical, metaphorical, and picturesque use of dialect (Jones 23–24).

As it was with the one-drop rule, black writers, such as Johnson, accepted inadvertently a link between black dialect and African American identity. Arguing that white writers distorted AAVE did not go far enough, however. What needed attacking was the larger assumption that language is an irreducible marker of racial identity. This presumed nexus fails to broach the most fundamental yet pressing questions: which regional black dialect is the "blacker," northern or southern, urban or rural? What could be explored about the semantic variations among urban dialects?

I am neither devaluing artistic and rhetorical uses of dialect nor disputing the economic, political, and social factors that have contributed to the formation and validation of dialects among African Americans. Rather, I am concerned with moves, direct or inadvertent, asserted by whites or blacks, that reinforce the triad of race, language, and ontology, codified from the late nineteenth to early twentieth century. In short, just as the literal speaking voice, concrete and measurable, became a metaphor for elusive and abstract presence in writing, the artistic use and misuse of black dialect contributed to the projection of collective black voice and consciousness.

Curiously, from the 1870s through the 1920s, some thinkers sought uniform respectability for edited American English. During this period, and most assuredly before, the British negatively viewed American English as a kind of nonstandard dialect. This is one of the reasons why Mencken wrote *The American Language*—to defend the linguistic integrity of American English. This almost incessant castigating of American English was further exacerbated by white America's struggle to codify what constituted "Americanness" in terms of cultural practices and traditions.

Because of the massive influx of immigrants to the United States, those like Mencken, who longed to privilege whatever was purely American, became more parochial in their definitions of American culture and language. European languages, which might distort the purity of American English, were to be rejected, and this curse, which had already befallen AAVE, intensified.

The standardized American English of this period and AAVE have something else in common. As literary critic Michael North argues, both bear a unique relationship to the development of artistic creativity. Just as Mark Twain believed his colloquial approach to dialogue and narrative to be more creative than Henry James's allegiance to refined, British syntax, black dialect became salient to the creative strategies of Modernism, a movement that stresses breaking away from the standard. North argues that not only Zora Neale Hurston, Langston Hughes, and white voyeurs of the Harlem Renaissance, such as Carl Van Vechten, but also T. S. Eliot, Gertrude Stein, and Wallace Stevens, to name a few, capitalized on the uninhibited creativity afforded by vernacular.

When North employs black voice, he is referring to the ways in which AAVE embodies the "destabilization" of standard language for artistic purposes. Moreover, North's arguments about black dialect are similar to those Eric Sundquist advances for AAVE and culture. First, the aural nuances of dialect cannot be captured in print, an argument Charles Chesnutt also made. Second, neither Euro-American culture nor Euro-American language exists apart from African American culture and dialect, and vice versa. Or to cite North, "the two races, the two languages, the two tongues are nonetheless inextricably joined. . . . [N]o matter how painfully Black and white may speak past one another, they are still linked" (pref.).

Black dialect, even more so than European languages brought to this country between the 1870s and 1920s, underscored the so-called purity of edited American English. As the color black had been juxtaposed with white since before the sixteenth century to illuminate the marked superiority of whiteness, so vernacular has through its assumed inferiority illustrated the superiority of the standardized discourse. Through the fray, however, the standard language has borrowed from vernacular in the same way mainstream culture has borrowed—sometimes intentionally, sometimes unintentionally—from African American vernacular culture. Even so, as some whites attempted to discard the *sordid* language and culture historically associated with African Americans, their hands, heads, and tongues were *soiled*.

Ann Douglas's reading of the evolution of American culture is likewise worth considering for its implications for vernacular and standardized language. Douglas refers to the intersection of white and black cultures during the 1920s as a process of "mongrelization." Strains of each distinct culture were bred into one another, so that what one typically perceived as pure white or pure black culture never existed in America. According to Douglas, neither white nor black culture might have been fully aware of this mongrelization. The reasons may have varied from the cultural elitists, nationalists, or racists who were repulsed by the idea (hence why Douglas adopts *mongrel*) to those who believed that the process of cultural hybridity was a long-range goal—social and political advancement would eventually result in integration. Similarly, the many ways standardized and colloquial dimensions of language reciprocally influence each other often went unnoticed.

In sum, I borrow the word *excesses* from Charles T. Davis to describe my evaluation of the use of the historically restricted definitions of blackness and dialect to demarcate racialized voice. To an extent, these boundaries and, subsequently, racialized voice are necessary rhetorically and unavoidable materially. But this should not be a rationale for even accepting implicitly the next step—that race is an irreducible element of identity, art, and language.

The Harlem Renaissance: Watershed of Color Consciousness

But if the African American's dark skin and other so-called Negroid physical characteristics, principally dialect, were deemed outward signs of the inward person, what about those classified as black who did not possess these traits? In other words, what about mixed-race persons who looked and sounded "white"? Certainly, their existence should have exposed the fallacy of attaching complexion to disposition.

Philosopher Naomi Zack and sociologist F. James Davis agree that from the second half of the nineteenth century through the 1920s, the one-drop rule became enshrined. For both, many factors contributed to this reality, including the backlash by southern whites against the 1875 civil rights legislation and their increasing intolerance of miscegenation.

Southern whites responded to the legislation by establishing Jim Crow codes. Perhaps the most relevant legislation for my discussion is *Plessy v. Ferguson*.[7] Homer Plessy, of one-eighth African ancestry, was the plaintiff in the trial that resulted in the 1896 "separate but equal" ruling. Although Plessy was to all appearances white, he was declared legally black, thus further codifying the one-drop rule.

During the 1920s, America's race construct received at once its greatest challenge and most significant reinforcement. One way Zack mounts her attack against the one-drop rule is to cite the celebrated anthropologist Franz Boas. As Zack reflects, Boas's research on race and culture was avant-garde.

> It wasn't until the 1920s that Franz Boas's efforts to distinguish between biological heredity and acquired culture began to break down the old theory that blood was the carrier of cultural characteristics. . . . His insistence that the differences in mental ability and vitality within each race were as great as the differences between the "average types" of each race was a crucial attack on the old blood theory of culture. (121–22)

Boas's work presented among the first scholarly objections to racist formulations of culture in America. His research exposed the assumptions of pseudobiology and pseudopsychology. Still, Zack does not believe Boas's theories went far enough. They should have exposed the rub for the one-drop rule: the existence of biracial persons. If, as Zack argues, black and white were truly dichotomous categories, then mixed-race people could not exist (97).

But Zack's critique of Boas ignores his discipline-specific objectives. Boas was an anthropologist, not a philosopher. And even though his work might have implications for philosophy, Zack's chiding him for not arguing like a philosopher is problematic. Boas's work gives us more to celebrate than to criticize. On the other hand, Boas could be criticized quantitatively and qualitatively for his inductive approach to studying nonwhite cultures. This approach entails the same possibility for hasty generalizations as the deductive approaches employed by his opponents. Both could result in applying conclusions drawn from one nonwhite culture to another culture of the same racial or ethnic background.

Nevertheless, many factors obviously contributed to the solidifying of the one-drop rule during the 1920s. But I am most interested in the role F. James Davis and Zack think the Harlem Renaissance writers played in this process. Davis offers two dates, 1915 and 1925, that he believes are pivotal for at least two reasons. First, both bear a direct relationship to black and white America's full acceptance of the one-drop rule, that the evidence of remote black ancestry renders one "black," irrespective of one's appearance. Second, the dates pinpoint transitions related to the Harlem Renaissance. "By 1915, white America, including the New Orleans and Charleston areas, had accepted the one-drop rule completely" (F. Davis 58). By approximately 1925, African Americans of all racial mixtures had done the same, "convinced that no alternative definition was possible."

Davis does not mention that Booker T. Washington also died in 1915. As a result, the mantle of black leadership needed an heir. Washington's younger nemesis, W. E. B. Du Bois, picked up this mantle, altering the course of the African American movement of the time from industrial self-help and political submission to classical education, black art as propaganda, and an assertive civil rights philosophy. These issues constitute some of the central debates of the Harlem Renaissance, with Du Bois as a major spokesperson. For my purposes, black art as propaganda is the most relevant debate, since I am questioning what constitutes blackness to begin with. Furthermore, the Harlem Renaissance was well under way by 1925.

For Davis, the Harlem Renaissance "symbolized" the evolution "of a new American black culture" and gave blacks "a sense of identity and group pride" (58). And this "new identity" was formed to defend the group against the negative images projected by white racists and black "extremists" like Marcus Garvey.

Born in Jamaica, Garvey came to Harlem in 1916 and became the leader of the Back to Africa movement. Convinced that blacks could never achieve full equality in America, Garvey raised millions of dollars to purchase ships to take his followers back to Africa. Some other African American leaders, such as Du Bois, wrote Garvey off as a fanatic, and Garvey considered Du Bois an ineffectual pawn for the white man. Be that as it may, Davis oversimplifies the case with Garvey. True, blacks wanted to create their own positive image; however, in keeping with their

interest in African roots (an interest Davis acknowledges), some prominent writers, such as poet and novelist Claude McKay, adopted Garvey's
nationalistic vision for a time.

Zack, on the other hand, criticizes the Harlem Renaissance writers
for strengthening the one-drop rule. Zack believes that these artists contributed inadvertently to the exclusion of mixed-race people who might
have chosen to be identified with both races of their heritage. In other
words, the Harlem Renaissance writers took advantage of one opportunity ("visibly mixed-race blacks and visibly white race blacks threw
in their lot with apparently pure-race blacks") while disregarding another opportunity: namely, dismantling the white-black racial hierarchy
(ch. 10).

Zack's reading of race during the Harlem Renaissance entails several
assumptions, the main being the wholesale adoption of the one-drop rule
by these artists. However, this was not the case. A number of prominent
writers during this period, including but not limited to Jessie Fauset, Jean
Toomer, and Nella Larsen, creatively and critically questioned the arbitrary line between black and white.[8] Further, as Zack partly concedes,
it is presumptuous to look back on the profound racism blacks suffered
during this period and then second-guess what the writers should have
done (99).

Zack alludes to but does not defend outright the need for African
Americans, during the 1920s, to express their worth to mainstream
America. In the minds of most of these artists, this goal would be best
accomplished by a group rather than by individuals. Hence, we have the
projection of the Harlem Renaissance as a united racial-cultural movement. I use the word *projection* because the Harlem Renaissance was
anything but the collective voice of African America; it was instead a
cacophony of dissenting voices.

In a series of lectures entitled *Race Contacts and Interracial Relations,*
Alain Locke, the reputed dean of the Harlem Renaissance, shows why
the projection of black unity, or more accurately, a collective ethos, was
necessary for the movement. Although biologically race is a fiction,
contends Locke, practically race can contribute to collective sociopolitical advancement. Locke's view predates Jacques Derrida's assertion
that one can recognize the use-value of a concept without accepting the
"truth-value" of that concept.[9] Although Locke's theory suggests an

agreed-upon strategy, the strategy itself places no stress on the fluidity of race constructions and, thereby, the possibility for reformulating definitions of group identity along racial lines.

To an extent, Zack's criticism of the Harlem Renaissance is legitimate. If in fact these writers projected American racial constructions as objective realities, were they not also projecting a restricted definition of racial identity and authorship? Is such a move further exacerbated by the larger-scale yet parallel efforts to define American identity during the 1870s through the 1920s? Before answering these questions, two tasks remain. First, I will review a few critical works from the Harlem Renaissance that represent cacophonous efforts to define collective identity and voice. Second, I will discuss how dialect was employed to demarcate black ontology.

Considering the selected works of four authors from the period will illustrate the first point. To begin with, "The New Negro" was the initial call to arms for the movement. Written in 1925 by Alain Locke, the essay sets the tone for the first major anthology of the Harlem Renaissance. As the title indicates, this essay praises blacks that break with the stereotypes associated with their race.

> In the last decade something beyond the watch and guard of statistics has happened in the life of the American Negro and the three norns who have presided over the Negro problem have a changeling in their laps. The Sociologist, the Philanthropist, the Race-leader are not unaware of the New Negro, but they are at a loss to account for him. He simply cannot be swathed in their formulae. For the younger generation is vibrant with a new psychology; the new spirit is awake in the masses, and under the very eyes of the professional observers is transforming what has been a perennial problem into the progressive phases of contemporary Negro life. (3)

Locke's essay develops from two major premises. First, there is a spirit "awake" in the younger blacks. And second, the self-designated friends of blacks cannot explain why. This complexity leads Locke to the crux of his argument: one cannot account for the origin of the "New Negro" because the "old Negro" never existed. That is, this "stock figure," who was "more a formula than a human being," was a myth to begin with.

Indeed, the old racial image had been "perpetuated as an historical fiction" both by whites, who either "condemned or defended" blacks, and by the African American who maintained "a sort of protective social mimicry forced upon him by the adverse circumstances of dependence" (3). Tragically, even "[t]he thinking Negro has been induced to share this same general attitude, to focus his attention on controversial issues, to see himself in the distorted perspective of a social problem" (3, 4).

Next, Locke incorporates a series of chronological examples that are designed to illustrate how the New Negro is not so new after all. To realize their promise, blacks must experience a "reorientation of view." Privileging the North and the South "on a sectional axis," they had "not noticed the East." For it is in the East, by which Locke means Harlem, that those blacks could come to appreciate the cultural richness of the spirituals (4). It is in the East that black migrants would learn that their identities were not confined to their former relationship to the South. By referring to Harlem as the East, Locke localizes the global metaphor of the East as the region of sagacity.

Further, Locke realizes that the movement from the South to Harlem is northward. But more than the geography of the Great Migration encompasses his rhetorical intent. The migration typified the move from the "countryside to the city," from "medieval America to modern" (6). This modernity stems from the "many diverse elements of Negro life" represented in Harlem, a diversity that ran the spectrum of class, region, and nationality. Thereby, Harlem became a microcosm for American democracy (12).

Locke's "New Negro" exposes the chasm between the perception and reality of African American culture. What gives me pause is not this project but how Locke seeks to achieve it. To bridge this chasm, blacks must develop a "wider race consciousness" (14). Unlike the race consciousness discussed by African American leaders of the past generation, this new consciousness would be international in scope.

Neither pan-Africanism nor the formation of a local group identity for political purposes, however, fully speaks to the limitations of this essay. Although the essay describes solidarity among blacks as a socially, politically, and artistically beneficial move, there are moments that open a space to covertly affirm racial essence. Phrases such as "group psychology" and "the mind of . . . a racial group" are especially telling in this regard. These concepts are perfectly acceptable, even valuable, if we are reminded that they are constructed. After all, a concept is a construct, not a brute fact. However, Locke seemingly closes his piece with a fairly conclusive, rather than tentative, perception of collective race consciousness.

While Locke admits the difficulty of achieving black solidarity, describing the process as "race welding" (7), he glosses over the complexities of diversity that region, class, and nationality, not to mention individual point of view, can foster. It is, therefore, ironic that like other members of the Talented Tenth, Locke castigates Marcus Garvey's Back to Africa movement as "transient" and "spectacular." As Garvey assumes that blacks of differing nationalities could easily unite if they returned to Mother Africa, Locke similarly assumes that a collective identity for all blacks was representable, if not achievable, in Harlem.

Further, Locke may be guilty of an inversion of the essentialism for which he chides other "race leaders" at the beginning of the essay. They were baffled because they could not understand the New Negro. Locke, a Harvard-educated philosopher and Rhodes scholar, presumes to both understand the New Negro and to articulate definitively a racially informed aesthetic code (15, 16).

Approximately one year after the publication of "The New Negro," journalist and satirist George S. Schuyler penned his most famous essay, "The Negro-Art Hokum." He argues clearly that what one typically thinks of as black art has more to do with class, region, and chronology than with color. He starts developing this thesis by referring to contributions blacks made in three areas: music, painting, and sculpture. So-called "Negro" music, from slave songs to spirituals, from the blues to jazz (an "outgrowth of ragtime") "are contributions of a caste in a certain section of the country" (Schuyler 51). In fact, these types of music are foreign to "Northern Negroes," "West Indian Negroes," and "African Negroes."

Schuyler introduces his ideological clincher when he says, "Any group under similar circumstances would have produced something similar" (51–52). Moving along the same line of reasoning, he suggests that the "literature, painting, and sculpture of the Aframericans," like that produced by whites, "shows more or less evidence of European influence." W. E. B. Du Bois, Meya Warick Fuller, and Henry Ossawa Tanner, for instance, were directly influenced by Europeans (52). It is, therefore, questionable at best to claim that the artistic contributions of "Aframericans" are "expressive of the Negro soul."

Schuyler's introduction of Aframerican is significant. Used by James Weldon Johnson, among others, the word privileges the Americanness of blacks over their African ancestry. This move is essential for Schuyler's next point: "your American Negro is just plain American." Given the same education and economic circumstances, "Negroes and whites from the same localities in this country talk, think, and act about the same" (52). Even the black newspapers, aside from "a slight dash of racialistic seasoning," are written in "good Americanese." Similarly, the works of Paul Laurence Dunbar, Charles Chesnutt, and James Weldon Johnson, like European artists of color, "show the impress of nationality rather than race."

Schuyler's essay enhances my analysis on at least two levels. In the first place, by critiquing the position that any work could be "expressive of the Negro soul," he debunks what I conceive to be an inverted form of race essentialism some blacks began positing, perhaps unintentionally, during the Harlem Renaissance. Second, he demonstrates the instability of race as an irreducible marker of identity, reminding his readers on the most fundamental phenotypic level that the African American's "color . . . ranges from dark brown to *pink*" (52, emphasis added).

This observation predates Schuyler's masterwork of satire, *Black No More*. In that novel, a black physician invents a formula that visibly transforms blacks into whites. Except for one woman, all other blacks, including the race leaders, use the formula. Terrified by the popular use of the formula and the prospect of widespread miscegenation, two white supremacist organizations (one ironically led by the protagonist, a former black man) try to find out who the imitation whites are. The artificial whites turn out to be lighter than the real ones. *Black No More* is Schuyler's testament to Americans' obsession with color. And like his essay, it discredits stereotypes about blacks.

On the other hand, Schuyler's essay understates the formidable impact of racism on the formation of American culture and letters. For example, he mentions Bert Williams (one of the first black minstrels) as one stereotype whites have accepted. Yet Williams created his stage characters according to the restrictions imposed by whites who had controlled the minstrel show industry since the mid-nineteenth century.[10] In the same way, Schuyler mentions the long-time heavyweight champion Jack Johnson, whom whites despised because he blatantly disrespected them and flagrantly maintained affairs with white women—actions that were not only antithetical to the "good darkie" image but could get a black person killed.

Most curious of all, Schuyler dismisses the influence of widely respected race theorists like Madison Grant and Lothrop Stoddard. Schuyler places quotation marks around the title *scientists* in order to diminish their credibility. Perhaps this approach enhances the quasi-satirical tone Schuyler wishes to maintain. But what is sacrificed in the process? A graduate of Columbia and Yale, Madison Grant wrote *The Passing of the Great Race* in 1916. Using Darwinism, he claimed that

> whites had physically evolved to such a specialized level of mental, moral, and social organization that they were vulnerable to mixture with "lower" races. . . . [T]he result of white and non-white racial mixing would always be a race reverting to the "lower race" in evolutionary specialization. (qtd. in Zack 100)

Grant's position went virtually unchallenged until World War II.[11] Writing during the 1920s, Lothrop Stoddard concurred with Grant, affirming that "the quality of the one-time largely Nordic population was being drastically lowered by mixture with 'inferior races'" (qtd. in F. Davis, 27).

Surely Schuyler must have been aware of the currency of these beliefs, which is undoubtedly why he alludes to them. Satire aside, Schuyler detracts today's readers from the ubiquity of the racism of his time. I have provided a cursory history of "scientific" racism to underscore how integral it is to understanding American culture generally and African American culture specifically. The fact that whites overall found it next to impossible to accept blacks like Ida B. Wells-Barnett and W. E. B. Du Bois as intellectually equal with whites, their academic training and civic participation notwithstanding, illuminates how blackness as the sign of inborn stupidity has been impressed upon the American psyche. Calling these individuals "exceptional" does not help matters either, for as the number of exceptions increased, one drop of black blood remained the genetic sign of inferiority.

Schuyler either misunderstood or simply missed the point that even the word *American* is coded white. Before, during, and since the Harlem Renaissance, whites, generally speaking, would not think of an African American when they heard the phrase "great American writer." Still further, asserting that like European blacks, American blacks are more influenced by a national vision than a racial one does not adequately advance Schuyler's position.

This portion of Schuyler's essay concludes with the implication that white cultural norms are more in keeping with this national vision than are black cultural norms. A white person politely applauding and mumbling "bravo" at an opera would probably come across as more quintessentially American to Schuyler than would a black parishioner fervently applauding and shouting "amen" after listening to the spirituals.

But Langston Hughes would see this point differently. Hailed as the manifesto of the Harlem Renaissance, his essay "The Negro Artist and the Racial Mountain" appeared just one week after Schuyler's. Predictably, it contests many of Schuyler's conclusions about race and art. For Hughes, race, not nationality or class, is the common denominator for the black artist. Like Schuyler's, Hughes's proposition can be easily summarized, especially because of the concrete, controlling metaphor he employs. Black artists must climb the mountain of racial inferiority and descend into a comfortable identification with the culture, manners, and traditions of all their people. Then these artists can ascend the mountain of racial pride.

By using the mountain metaphor, Hughes illuminates how substantive race is to the artistic enterprise. Race is not incidental, as Schuyler contends. Similar to Locke, Hughes clings to a type of racial psychology. He argues that black artists should not be afraid to use black folk culture. According to Hughes, the African American artist can demonstrate such fear in many ways but chiefly by statements such as "I want to be a poet—not a Negro poet" (55). He goes on to demonstrate how this same poet will use his middle-class background as an excuse to ignore the more common elements of black life as source material. For Hughes, not even fear must inhibit the black artist's free choice. This observation dovetails into the central declaration of the essay:

> We younger Negro artists who create now intend to express
> our individual dark-skinned selves without fear or shame. If

white people are pleased we are glad. If they are not, it doesn't matter. We know that we are beautiful and ugly too. The tom-tom cries and the tom-tom laughs. If colored people are pleased we are glad. If they are not, their displeasure doesn't matter either. We build our temples for tomorrow, strong as we know how, and we stand on top of the mountain, *free* within ourselves. (59, emphasis added)

This passage captures the ideal of artistic freedom: be true to your vision. It also poses a postmodern question: can a text written by a black artist exist in isolation? Realistically, could Hughes's dream of black artists writing in spite of the possible disapproval of whites or other blacks be realized?

Indeed, many African American writers during the Harlem Renaissance had white patrons. If most of these patrons, like Hughes's Mrs. Mason, demanded significant revisions in their charges' work, how completely could these artists (including Hughes) apply the bold words of the above declaration? The same could be asked of white publishers or, more important, elite black artists who wished to impose their restrictions on other, lesser-known black artists.

And Hughes qualifies as one of those elite black artists. Of course he questioned mandates from older-generation Harlem intellectuals, such as Alain Locke and W. E. B. Du Bois, who wanted black writers to portray blacks only in a positive light. But as his essay develops, Hughes subscribes to the philosophy he challenges. If the overriding issue is the writer's freedom, could not the black writer write about something other than black life? This decision could be a sign that this writer deems African American culture to be inferior, but is this necessarily the case?

Related to this idea is the way Hughes constructs the identity of the black artist. Before proclaiming how the younger black writers would express their "dark-skinned selves," he praises four such artists, one of whom, Jean Toomer, was not dark-skinned. Neither was Chesnutt, whom Hughes discusses earlier. Hughes seemed surprisingly more certain about Toomer's racial identity than was Toomer himself.[12]

The most problematic moments in the essay are when Hughes employs descriptions of other African American artists that, although perhaps employed rhetorically, still project problematic generalizations about race. A black artist, for instance, can "run away spiritually from his race" (Hughes 55). Toomer's *Cane* and Paul Robeson's singing are "truly racial" (58). Hughes hopes for a group of black painters who will "create with new technique the expressions of their own soul-world." And finally, "jazz" is listed among other things as "distinctly racial" (58).

As I alluded earlier, Nella Larsen's work forcefully complicates the distinctions integral to America's color line. Yet Larsen makes this move by expanding the psychology of identity to encompass gender as well as race and class markers. Her two short novels, *Quicksand* and *Passing,* along with the marginalization she suffered during her controversial career, illustrate the heightened material realities a woman of color faced in the seemingly existential and abstract act of constructing public and personal identity during the Harlem Renaissance.

Deborah McDowell opines that through the protagonists in both *Quicksand* and *Passing,* Larsen explicates the complex "psychic dualism" that lay behind the material realities of racism, sexism, and classicism. Helga Crane, in *Quicksand,* and Clare and Irene, in *Passing,* are forced onto the borders, trapped in the ambivalent dualities of all the identity markers just mentioned. They are light enough to pass for white but realize that they can never be truly white. They desire sexual and material autonomy but adhere, or in the case of Clare and Irene, appear to adhere to the marital conventions that traditionally delimit both sexuality and class status.

The female characters in Larsen's novels experience a Du Boisian double consciousness that, to borrow from Shirley Wilson Logan's language, "converges and diverges" from race. Put another way, Larsen's personal life represents her own struggle along the lines of race, gender, and class. Born of a Danish mother and a West Indian father, she felt that she could not fully identify with either blacks or whites. Through her writing, she sought the financial and personal autonomy that should accompany authorship, yet she married a well-respected physicist in part to secure her place as a middle-class woman.

Hence, what McDowell views as the key to understanding Larsen's characters, Thadious M. Davis deems the approach to understanding Larsen's creation of authorial ethos. For Davis, Larsen's constructed authorial ethos correlates with the persona she projected in her private life.

Locke's, Schuyler's, Hughes's, and Larsen's respective writings nonetheless introduce the fundamental quandary for Harlem Renaissance artists: projecting a racially unified movement or collective ethos while maintaining individual artistic freedom. The first impulse involves one seemingly accepting a flawed definition of race to achieve unity; the second seeks to resist all restrictions, including those inscribed for the sake of racial solidarity.

Race as a Way of Reading

Since an exclusively phenotypic reading of race, specifically "blackness," is not sound theoretically, what should be employed in its place? As I suggested at the beginning of this chapter, ascertaining what constitutes blackness, however tentatively, is a necessary prerequisite to determining the nature of black voice. Henry Louis Gates Jr., among other scholars, has replaced a literal conceptualization of race with a metaphorical one.

Although most of Gates's scholarship in this area has reference to literary criticism and not authorship in composition theory, he edits one study that has telling implications for composition.[13] Still, all of Gates's major texts, *Figures in Black: Words, Signs and the "Racial" Self; The Signifying Monkey; "Race," Writing, and Difference; Loose Canons: Notes on the Culture Wars;* and *The Future of the Race,* the last coauthored with Cornel West, point to the same metaphors as a refrain (even when these metaphors are not mentioned specifically): race is a text; race is a trope.

Surely Gates adopts these metaphors to move away from static racial designations and their attending ideological baggage. "Trope" literally means a "twisting in the wind," connoting indeterminacy. Likewise, a text can be read from an infinite array of viewpoints. Gates would not want us to conclude, however, that because race is neither concrete nor static, it is therefore meaningless. On the contrary, his retort would parallel the analogy Kwame Anthony Appiah uses to rebut those who criticize him for calling race a myth: witches did not have to exist in seventeenth-century Massachusetts for women to be burned at the stake.

Nevertheless, Gates's metaphors entail some of the same fallacies as literal takes on race. Like the literal perceptions of blackness reviewed in this chapter, Gates's metaphors focus on race itself rather than on how race works. That is to say, race becomes the object of analysis or "reading." Whether one is talking about complexion, the one-drop rule, or Gates's text and trope, the common ground remains reading race.

At least two consequences arise for Gates: First, although he avoids a literal interpretation of race, he does so at the expense of ascribing materiality to an abstraction (race) rather than the primarily material effects of that abstraction. And by so doing, his metaphors may not afford him the flexibility in defining race that he desires. Second, these metaphors may also minimize the importance of blackness in American social history. To objectify race, whether through literal or metaphorical readings, then, delimits the object of interpretation. The focus becomes blackness, and not blackness as it interacts with American culture and society more broadly.

Instead of objectifying race by means of either literal readings adopted throughout history or the metaphorical readings Gates and others espouse, I opt to subjectify race, particularly blackness, in relationship to the broader American cultural landscape. I am using *subjectify* in two senses here: personally—in terms of agency—and communally—in terms of cultural affiliation. Referring to race as a "cultural hermeneutic," while clearly constructed and tentative, is nonetheless comprehensive enough to affirm the fluidity of race without devaluing its personal and cultural import.

Designating race as a cultural hermeneutic envisions race not as something to be read but as a *way of reading*. This distinction emphasizes racialized constructions as matters of agency, willful or imposed, corporate or individual. Race as a way of reading further evinces the fluidity of race in reference to the process of interpretation as well as the multitude of interpreters.

Race as a cultural hermeneutic, then, is a fitting operative phrase, for as this chapter has demonstrated, America's preoccupation with race has informed its intellectual history. Construing race in this way may be a beginning approach to balancing the theoretical critique of the American race construct (scholars such as Kwame Anthony Appiah posit) with the material concerns about contemporary racism within and without the academy.

To some degree, Appiah sees the canonization of African American letters as an insidious inversion of the Eurocentrism that has characterized American letters in general. The issue for Appiah is not whether we should include texts written by those called "black" or "African American" but rather how this inclusion, if motivated primarily by race, reinforces what proponents of multiculturalism seek to discredit; namely, race as a determinant of literary value.

Houston Baker, conversely, believes that Appiah begs two key issues: first, the right of a group of people to define themselves by their own terms, "traditions," and art; and second, what he calls the "taxi fallacy." Baker introduces the difficulties black men in New York confront when trying to catch a cab to exemplify the practical irrelevance of projects like Appiah's; or as Du Bois surmised over fifty years earlier, "the Black man is a person who must ride 'Jim Crow' in Georgia."

Similarly, in *Playing in the Dark,* Toni Morrison offers a political rationale for avoiding the trap of assuming race no longer matters, a conclusion that could be drawn from Appiah's position. Morrison argues that the push toward the colorlessness of the Western tradition aesthetic represents the same hegemonic power that established racial boundaries to begin with. In light of the designation "cultural hermeneutic," Appiah's, Baker's, and Morrison's arguments need not be mutually exclusive. On the contrary, one can assert that race and voice are constructions without dismissing their private and public significance.

Race as a cultural hermeneutic does not provide closure in reading American society. What seems to separate this theory from Gates's is that he is interested in the play of language itself. The focus should be on meaning, however tentative or varied, that can be ascribed to American society by employing race as a way of reading that society. American society, instead of race, becomes the text. My project, then, only suggests closure insofar as the American versions of cultural hermeneutics can be tailored to our rhetorical benefit.

Racialized voice can be an agreed-upon strategy for establishing community, subject to revision or remaking, but an approach nonetheless.

3

Chesnutt's Reconstruction of Race and Dialect

CHESNUTT IS A FASCINATING FIGURE WITH WHOM to begin a reconsideration of racialized voice, to begin thinking through race as a way of reading American culture and constructing authorial ethos. In the first place, his literary career nearly spans the historical period surveyed in this book, although he was more active from the 1880s through the early 1900s and produced fewer writings during and after the Harlem Renaissance. His better-known writings began appearing in 1887, when the *Atlantic Monthly* published "The Goophered Grapevine," the first serial installment of Chesnutt's conjure tales. These better-known writings end with *The Colonel's Dream* in 1905.

In the second place, Chesnutt was recognized by many, W. E. B. Du Bois among them, as the father of the Harlem literary movement. Most engaging are the ways in which Chesnutt's life and writings question America's race binary. Indeed, revisiting Chesnutt's thinking could significantly inform current biracial or multiracial student writers' existential and social struggles with constructing their authorial identities along the axis of black and white. Similarly, teachers of writing could begin formulating composition theory and pedagogy, based on a critical reading of Chesnutt, which is more sensitive to the needs of our racially mixed students.

To all appearances white, Chesnutt accepted the title of "Negro writer." In a brief article for the *Crisis,* shortly after Chesnutt's death, Du Bois wrote,

Charles Waddell Chesnutt, genial American gentleman and
dean of Negro literature in this land, is dead. . . . Chesnutt
was of that group of white folk who because of a more or
less remote Negro ancestor identified himself voluntarily with
the darker group, studied them, expressed them, defended
them, yet never forgot the absurdity of this artificial position
and always refused to admit its logic or its ethical sanction.
He was not a Negro; he was a man. ("Chesnutt")

Du Bois interprets accurately Chesnutt's disdain for the "artificial
position" inscribed on the African American's existence and based on
inconclusive racial categories. But Du Bois ignores or remains silent on
the extent of Chesnutt's critique when he calls Chesnutt a "white man."
Chesnutt was not so sure. One of his journal entries, dated July 31, 1875,
attests to this uncertainty:

Twice today, or oftener, I have been taken for "white." At the
pond this morning one fellow said he'd "be damned if there
were any nigger blood in me." At Coleman's I passed. On the
road an old chap, seeing the trunks, took me for a student
coming from school. I believe I'll leave here and pass anyhow,
for I am as white as any of them. One old fellow said today,
"Look here, Tom. Here's a black fellow as white as you are."
(Brodhead, *Journals*)

One similarity between this passage and the one written by Du Bois is
that Chesnutt, in keeping with Du Bois's assessment of him, utilized
personal choice to construct his racial identity. Du Bois says Chesnutt
chose to be black; here the young Chesnutt claims that he occasionally
chose to pass for white. Arguably, Chesnutt did not usually pass. As
Frances Richardson Keller suggests, Chesnutt found it practically beneficial to pass while he traveled. And he would continue this practice
several years after he, at seventeen, wrote the above journal entry. However, he often confronted discrimination when his wife Susan, darker
than he, traveled with him (Keller 228).

So why incorporate the personal musings of the seventeen-year-old
Chesnutt to complicate Du Bois's memorial for the seventy-four-year-
old literary giant? The reason is simple. Chesnutt's vision of his racial
identity did not change that much over fifty years. True enough, he did

not consider himself white, but neither did he consider himself black. Four years before his death and twenty-three years after the publication of *The Colonel's Dream,* the NAACP honored Chesnutt with the coveted Spingarn Medal. During his reception speech, he said,

> [S]ubstantially all of my writings, with the exception of *The Conjure Woman,* have dealt with the problems of people of mixed blood, which, while in the main the same as those of the true Negro, are in some instances and in some respects more complex and difficult of treatment, in fiction as in life. (Rpt. in Gibson 126)

More important to Chesnutt than his writing was his positioning of mixed race as a distinct category. In fact, as the above citation makes clear, it was this larger desire for a racial identity other than black or white that informed his crafting of fiction and nonfiction. This is one reason why many of Chesnutt's short stories adhere to the Euro-American genteel tradition while highlighting the value of African American cultural traditions, like conjure.[1] Incorporating the cultural aspects of both racial identities mirrored the sense of in-betweenness he desired.

Even William L. Andrews remarks of Chesnutt, "[H]e was the first African American writer to enlist the white controlled publishing industry in the service of his social message" and "has been increasingly recognized as a literary innovator whose mastery of his craft, particularly in the short story, placed his distinctive personal signature on the pages of American literary history" (Introduction vii). While Andrews surmises the unique impact of Chesnutt's writings, he assumes, as did Du Bois sixty years earlier, a racial classification for Chesnutt that Chesnutt rejected. This illustrates the contemporary need to explain the rationale behind Chesnutt's reconstruction of race.

Chesnutt chose not to acknowledge publicly his African ancestry until after his first collection of short stories, *The Conjure Woman,* which appeared in March 1899, received rave reviews. Chesnutt avoided mentioning race from the start of his career because he wanted *The Conjure Woman* to "be read and reviewed on its own without regard to the racial antecedents of its author."[2]

Throughout his career, Chesnutt occasionally "refers indirectly to himself as a 'Negro' or 'colored' but never directly" (Gibson 126). When trying to ascertain Chesnutt's perspective on passing, for instance, one should bear in mind his belief in the absurdity of America's limited racial designations; the material benefits he might glean from racialized social customs were important but secondary.[3]

Paradoxically, the stellar reviews Chesnutt received for his short stories, particularly "The Wife of His Youth" and "The Conjure Woman," contributed to his emergence as a spokesperson for the black race.[4] In May of 1900, the critic William Dean Howells wrote an article for the *Atlantic Monthly* that praised Chesnutt for his "technical skill and literary imagination" (Heermance 89). Howells mentioned Chesnutt's race but emphasized his artistry.

Not surprisingly, the social climate that would move some of Howells's readers to maximize what Howells wished to minimize (Chesnutt's race) was already being fostered one year earlier. Impressed by both the success of Chesnutt's two most famous short stories, editor M. A. DeWolfe invited Chesnutt to write a biography of Frederick Douglass. J. Noel Heermance notes the significance of Chesnutt's acceptance:

> The invitation to write this biography, and the biography itself, now formed the first tangible recognition by American publishers of Chesnutt's status as a black spokesperson. This recognition was to spread rapidly. (91)

Douglass was one of the men whom Chesnutt most admired. Douglass personified the individualism, self-education, and middle-class work ethic that both men accepted as requisite for achieving the American Dream. Chesnutt lived out this dream. An exceptional author, he also received one of the highest scores on the Ohio bar examination, though he never practiced law, and ran a successful stenography business. In the same way, both Douglass and Chesnutt had thrust upon them the burden of racial spokesperson. During Chesnutt's life, however, Booker T. Washington and, later, W. E. B. Du Bois were more popularly associated with that position. But perhaps the literary public, among several others, regarded Chesnutt as the true spokesperson instead.

Whatever the case, Chesnutt does part company with Douglass in rejecting the race binary. Douglass challenged America's race hierarchy but merely flirted with the in-between space that Chesnutt embraced through positing mixed race. Whereas Douglass's stance toward America's racial categories in and of themselves can be styled as ambivalent, Chesnutt's can be described as reconstructive. Or to put the matter differently, where Douglass sought, in part because of racism, to integrate his inner and public voice, Chesnutt felt at ease shrewdly separating the two. Therefore, I must look upon Chesnutt's acceptance of the titles of Negro writer and racial spokesperson as, in part, projecting a rhetorical ethos. He longed for equality for the African American masses; yet, for the most part, neither these masses nor white Americans could fathom his effort to do so while transcending America's dichotomization of race.

Chesnutt's prose, then, reveals the artistic sophistication and the social consciousness of the first widely reputed "African American" fiction writer. His writing further foreshadows the problem of classifying a mixed-race writer with fixed designations like "white" or "black." One work in which Chesnutt clearly undertakes a critique of the construct of race itself is in his second short-story collection, published in the fall of the same year as the first. *The Wife of His Youth* parallels Naomi Zack's argument in *Race and Mixed Race*. Curiously, Zack concedes Chesnutt's recognition of mixed race yet ignores his critique of the one-drop rule. Since Zack's thesis hinges on the intimate connection between denying the one-drop rule and affirming mixed race, one wonders why she overlooked Chesnutt's treatment of that subject.

From the One-Drop Rule to a Mixed-Race Reality

Understanding Chesnutt's attack of the one-drop rule, then, is preliminary to understanding his positioning of mixed race. In fact, the first four stories in *The Wife of His Youth* address the one-drop rule, providing ideological scaffolding upon which the other stories could frame Chesnutt's tacit argument: mixed-race identity is a reality obfuscated by a biological myth that has constructed a counterreality.

Chesnutt opens the title story by introducing Mr. Ryder, a man who could easily pass for white. Furthermore, he clearly practices the elitist intraracism characteristic of his time. He, like his other light-skinned African American associates, deems social acceptance of his darker brethren a "backward step." With a description of Ryder's unexpected nighttime visitor, Chesnutt introduces the story's turning point: "And she was very black—so black that her toothless gums, revealed when she opened her mouth to speak, were not red, but blue" (Chesnutt, *Collected* 106).

The perceived savage appearance of the dark woman extends to every part of her body, presumably resulting from her neglect of oral hygiene, hence blue gums instead of red. Red is also the source of life, the evidence of vitality, the color of blood. At the beginning of the story, however, the word *blue* describes the "Blue Vein Society," an affluent group of mixed-race blacks whose skin was so light one could see their veins.

This woman turns out to be the long lost wife of the wealthy Mr. Ryder, and it is she, not the lovely mixed-race widow Mrs. Dixon, that Ryder chooses at the close of the narrative. More interesting is that Ryder makes this decision despite his elitist leanings that would socially proscribe such a union. In theory, honor emerges as the superlative attribute of Blue Vein Society members.

Likewise, the ostensibly white Clara Hohfelder from "Her Virginia Mammy" assumes that blacks are "darker and uncouth" than the mixed-race students she taught to dance (*Collected* 120). Although her belief reflects racial essentialism, such a belief is actually more logically consistent than is the one-drop rule. If "blackness" is the inherent mark of stupidity, perversity, and savagery, then the darker one is, the more one should manifest these flaws. To some degree, Clara shares the sentiments of her fiancé about the plight of her mixed-race students, "to be white yet to be classified as black—so close yet so far" (121).

Near the end of the story, Clara discovers that she had a black "mammy" when she was a child. She never discovers that this newly found mammy is her biological mother. Clara's new identity, uncovered in relationship to her mother, is created by her misperception. So it was with her former identity.

"The Sheriff's Children" provides still another dimension to the discussion of blood, race, and ancestral identity. Sheriff Campbell, bold enough to protect a black prisoner from lynching, is rendered virtually speechless when this prisoner reveals that he is the sheriff's bastard son. Campbell's near muteness escalates to terror when the prisoner, Tom, threatens to kill the sheriff with his own gun. Tom's reply to Campbell's question—"you would not murder your own father?"—is telling:

> It were well enough to claim the relationship, but it comes with poor grace from you to ask anything by reason of it. What father's duty have you ever performed for me? Did you give me your name or even your protection? (*Collected* 144)

When Campbell replies that he had given Tom life, Tom retorts: "What kind of life? You gave me your own blood, your own features . . . and you gave me a black mother" (144). Indeed, all characteristics including complexion, hair, and even knowledge of one's ancestry are nebulous determinants of racial identity. That Tom's father could choose to claim or reject him demonstrates on the most basic level why racialization is complex.

Similar to Mr. Ryder's observations in "The Wife of His Youth," Mr. Clayton's in "A Matter of Principle" show how intraracism may sometimes be, like covert forms of white racism, tempered with so-called liberal insight:

> "I know," he would say, "that white people lump us all together as negroes, and condemn all us to the same social ostracism. But I don't accept this classification, for my part, and I imagine that, as the chief party in interest, I have a right to my opinion. People who belong by half or more of their blood to the most virile and progressive race of modern times have as much right to call themselves white as others have to call themselves negroes." (Collected 149)

On the surface, denying the "black" side of one's heritage, as Clayton does, seems comparable to betraying one's relatives—and indeed in one sense, it may be. However, the question evoked by the passage—"Why couldn't a person of mixed-race heritage claim allegiance to whiteness as others claim allegiance to blackness?"—resonates as philosophically sound given the arbitrariness of racial categories.

The White Artist and Black Dialogue

To grasp the significance of Chesnutt's contribution to the literary use of black dialect, one must have, at the very least, an introduction to the thinking of two of Chesnutt's white contemporaries in dialect writing: Joel Chandler Harris and Thomas Nelson Page. The popularity of plantation fiction as a literary genre also must be borne in mind. I will briefly discuss Harris, the more popular of the two. Moreover, Chesnutt's plantation writings are most frequently compared to Harris's.[5]

Born in 1848, Harris was introduced to the press and southern plantation culture just a few miles from his hometown, Eatonton, Georgia.

While in his midteens, he became an apprentice printer for Joseph Addison Turner, owner and editor of the *Countryman*. Since Turner published the paper on his estate, Harris, limited by an elementary education, not only benefited from Turner's library but also heard the dialect and folk tales that he later attempted to reproduce in his *Uncle Remus Tales*.[6]

By 1876, after working over the years in various capacities for newspapers in Georgia and Louisiana, Harris became a writer for the *Atlanta Constitution*. Here his career began in earnest. Not long after Harris joined the *Constitution,* he was asked to take over a serial with a principal character named "Uncle Si." Recalling his experience on Turner's plantation, Harris opted instead for the name "Uncle Remus." And by 1880, J. C. Derby, a representative of Appleton Publishers of New York and one already familiar with the Uncle Remus sketches, paid Harris a visit that eventually led to the publishing of *Uncle Remus: His Songs and Sayings* in 1881.

The book consists of four major sections: "Legends of the Old Plantation," "His Songs," "A Story of the War," and "His Sayings." The largest section, "Legends of the Old Plantation," consists of animal tales, for which Uncle Remus is best known.[7] Additionally, the two main characters are Uncle Remus and a little boy, evidently the son of Uncle Remus's former master. All of Remus's tales, songs, and sayings are framed within a third-person narrative told by a white man. And this is one of the facts that leads to the question of the collection's authenticity.

Several sources attest to the authenticity of Harris's representation of dialect. Mark Twain, himself greatly skilled in the literary use of dialect, observed, "Mr. Harris ought to be able to read the Negro dialect better than anybody else, for in the matter of writing it he is the only master the country has produced" (rpt. in *Sandglass* 1).

Likewise, J. L. Dillard makes a number of favorable comments about Harris's work, including a possible syntactical connection between a phrase the trickster Brer Rabbit repeatedly uses and a West African phrase, an example of what Dillard calls "Africanisms" (121). More impressive is that respected African Americans, such as William Stanley Braithwaite and Sterling Brown, confirmed the cultural worth of Harris's tales.[8]

But probably the most colorful, though perhaps not the most convincing, testimony to the authenticity of Harris's work comes from a letter he penned to the *Folk-Lore Journal of London:*

It is a misfortune, perhaps, from an English point of view, that the stories in this volume are rendered in the American Negro dialect, but it was my desire to preserve the stories as far as I might be able in the form in which I heard them, and to preserve also if possible the quaint humor of the Negro. It is his humor that gives the collection its popularity in the United States, but I think you will find the stories more important than humorous should you take the trouble to examine them. Not one of them is cooked, and not one nor any part of one is an invention of mine. They are all genuine folk tales. (*Sandglass* 3)

A number of conflicts surface in this citation, but I mention only two here. The most obvious one arises between Harris the chronicler and Harris the author. Even if *Uncle Remus: His Songs and Sayings* were not replete with intrusions from the third-person narrator, Harris's earlier act of selecting the tales raises a question about the collection's authenticity.

Harris selected the tales he believed to be best representative of blacks. But is he qualified to make such a determination? In other words, he made choices that every writer has the right to make. Yet in the above letter, he seems to be trivializing these choices. Certainly, Mark Twain, George Washington Cable, and a host of other authors and publishers during and after Harris's life did not simply honor his ability to record black speech. They honored Harris mainly for his skill as a writer.

Assuredly, Harris's bias against AAVE comprises the more telling conflict. Black dialect is good enough to convey black folklore, if chronicled by a white writer of Harris's capabilities, but it is not good enough to stand on its own as a valid linguistic medium. That Mark Twain, for instance, also used black dialect in crafting the vernacular of his southern white characters indicates the fallacy of Harris's assumption.[9] Harris celebrated black dialect for the claim to authenticity that it afforded him yet despised this medium for what he perceived to be its linguistic limitations.

But Harris's book entails more pressing issues than either the linguistic accuracy of his representation of dialect or bias against it. Instead, the issue becomes, how does the book reify the connection made during the nineteenth century between black language and black being? This connection arrests Gates's attention as well:

After all, by 1895, dialect had come to connote black innate mental inferiority, the linguistic sign both of human bondage (as origin) and of the continued failure of "improvability" or "progress," two turn of the century key words. . . . [A]nd even sympathetic characterizations of the black, such as Uncle Remus by Joel Chandler Harris, were far more related to a racist textual tradition that stemmed from minstrelsy, the plantation novel, and vaudeville than to the representations of spoken language. (*Signifying* 176)

Gates is right and wrong about Harris. Harris was anything but "sympathetic" in his portrayal of black people. Other than ensuring the linguistic credibility that Harris needed to employ black dialect in his narrative, Uncle Remus serves no integral purpose. He is a stock character, a puppet through whom Harris mouths his restrictive take on the tales, songs, and sayings. John F. Callahan concurs when he notes that for "Harris, personality is static. Nothing happens to change Uncle Remus in character and outlook. He remains entirely consistent with Harris's initial ventriloquist portrait" (40).

Gates indicates correctly, however, that Harris believed his writings were a window into black consciousness. While conceding a difference between the dialect of the "tales" and "sayings" sections of his book, Harris claimed that he included the latter type of dialect "for the purpose of presenting a phase of Negro character wholly distinct from that which I have endeavored to preserve in the legends" (J. Harris viii). What Harris asserts cannot be achieved. "Character" is much too elusive to be coupled with "dialect." Language will fail to provide access, with any degree of certainty, to the collective temperament, personality, or virtues of a people, if such could be proven to exist at all.

Chesnutt on Dialect and Conjure

"Reconstruction" is also a fitting description for Chesnutt's work with dialect, specifically in *The Conjure Woman* short story collection. When I use the word *reconstruction,* I intend no pun related to the fact that Chesnutt begins his career after America's Reconstruction. On the contrary, I am claiming that Chesnutt altered existing epistemologies pertaining to the nexus among dialect, race, and identity without completely transcending these epistemologies.

Especially with language, Chesnutt does not dismantle the nineteenth-century hierarchy between standardized American English and AAVE. In *The Conjure Woman* tales, he does not altogether dispense with the pathos and humor range of literary dialect that James Weldon Johnson later decried. To be sure, Chesnutt appears to be paying homage to the dialect tradition represented in the plantation fiction of his white contemporaries, Joel Chandler Harris and Thomas Nelson Page.[10] However, in a letter he wrote to his editor, Walter Hines Page at Houghton-Mifflin, Chesnutt expresses a guarded skepticism about the existence of AAVE, asserting "there is no such thing as Negro dialect." Eric Sundquist clarifies that Chesnutt's skepticism was most likely due to his conviction that the aural nuances of dialect were not reproducible in print.

But this letter accentuates a larger axiom, one that Sundquist at best vaguely alludes to—through language we cannot gain access to the nuances of racial identity. And although one finds the orthographic distortions, as well as the limited scope of humor and pathos, common to other plantation fiction in *The Conjure Woman,* Chesnutt's reconstruction of dialect lies in his radical revision of its content rather than its structure.

The original edition of *The Conjure Woman* contained seven of Chesnutt's dialect stories. The principal characters are a white businessman John, his wife Annie, and an elderly ex-slave named Uncle Julius. In the hope of improving his wife's health, the couple migrates from northern Ohio to central North Carolina, where they meet and hire Uncle Julius. Most of the tales consist of Julius's reveries of the pre–Civil War South, and similar to Harris's *Uncle Remus,* a white person controls the narrative. John is the primary narrator; Julius is the secondary narrator. In contrast to the *Uncle Remus* tales, John is a character within the narrative.

As Richard Brodhead opines, there are other parallels between Chesnutt's and Harris's respective works, the most notable being Chesnutt's reverence for the southern aristocratic class. Chesnutt definitely wishes to communicate that Uncle Julius's white employers are "superior" to him, yet according to Donald Gibson, not "simply because he works for them or because they are considerably better off economically and speak better English. The difference is a class difference" (Gibson 129). Chesnutt also criticizes poor whites through Uncle Julius, who "had a profound contempt for them" ("A Deep Sleeper" in *Conjure* 137).

Notwithstanding the partial validity of Gibson's observation, Chesnutt does not romanticize the antebellum South to the extent that Harris or Page did.[11] Uncle Julius attests to the horrors of slavery. Particularly noteworthy, however, is how Uncle Julius dupes his educated, northern white employer with stories told in black dialect. This becomes pertinent, since Chesnutt identifies more with John than with Uncle Julius. Yet unlike his African American contemporary Paul Laurence Dunbar, Chesnutt did not have an enduring investment in black dialect.[12]

As I have already shown, Chesnutt's ideological investment was in the positioning of mixed race. A teacher at a Normal School for African American children in North Carolina, he taught black children to use edited American English, most likely disdaining their use of dialect. In fact, Chesnutt's mixed-race characters rarely use AAVE. Certainly this holds true with his novels from *Mandy Oxendine*[13] to *The Marrow of Tradition*. For Chesnutt, dialect is associated to some degree with class. These facts make Chesnutt's narrative take on dialect all the more intriguing.

In a few instances, John concedes the literary quality of Uncle Julius's dialect stories. Although John chides Uncle Julius for his ignorance, he also admires the old man's storytelling finesse. In several places throughout the tales, John muses over Julius's astounding facility with narrative, which the following passage from "The Gray Wolf's Ha'nt" illustrates:

> It was not difficult to induce the old man to tell a story, if he were in a reminiscent mood. Of the tales of the old slavery days he seemed indeed to possess an exhaustless store,—some weirdly grotesque, some broadly humorous; some bearing the stamp of truth, faint perhaps, but still discernible; others palpable inventions, whether his own or not we never knew, though his fancy doubtless embellished them. But even the wildest was not without an element of pathos,—the tragedy, it might be, of the story itself. (*Conjure* 96)

Through John, Chesnutt ascribes value to Uncle Julius's narrative. As a master storyteller, Julius possesses a wealth of sources and the ability to craft those sources. The word *pathos* might recall James Weldon Johnson's objection to pathos as one of the limited emotional elements employed in dialect literature. Within this context, however, John actually highlights how Uncle Julius's stories produce identification between teller and listener, not merely the listener's sympathy. Similarly, so taken is John by Julius's flair with imaginary stories that he ponders over "how many original minds, which might have added to the world's wealth of literature and art, had been buried in the oceans of slavery" (*Conjure* 148–49). To summarize, Uncle Julius "took the crude legends and vague superstitions of the neighborhood and embodied them in stories as complete, in their way, as the Sagas of Iceland or the primitive tales of ancient Greece" (196). Uncle Julius's "inferior" dialect does not inhibit his creativity. Surely, a part of John's astonishment about these tales comes from the fact that although Uncle Julius is ignorant (reflected presumably by his use of dialect), through the tales he surpasses John's expectations. He expected the old ex-slave to tell quaint, humorous stories. He received much more.

Of course, Chesnutt still privileges Eurocentrism, from revering the audience for these tales (obviously white) to predicating the value of Uncle Julius's narrative on John's positive assessment as well as its relationship to the larger, "master" narrative. As a linguistic medium for the secondary narrative, Chesnutt does not allow AAVE to transcend the confines of standardized American English, but he does afford dialect a greater degree of aesthetic freedom within those confines.

Moreover with the conjure tales, Chesnutt demonstrates the ambiguity of racialized voice by easily shifting from what could be styled white narrative voice to a black narrative voice, both types of public voice. The compelling manner in which Uncle Julius's dialect becomes essential to the narrative adds credence to these tales. Obviously, Chesnutt accomplishes this with John's narrative as well. Both are equally effective narrative constructions of dialogue, standard and nonstandard. Likewise, the interchange between the white primary narrator and the black secondary narrator enacts Chesnutt's greater and lesser regard for Euro-American genteel and African American folk traditions. For Callahan, this interchange of narrative voices captures how Chesnutt's tales differ from and surpass Harris's:

> In contrast to the formulaic, mechanical relationship between Uncle Remus and the little boy, the voices of Chesnutt's narrators, John and Uncle Julius, contend dynamically on the field of narrative. Chesnutt's frame keeps their personalities unfolding and not merely reiterative; subtly, and in the case

of John, unwillingly, each becomes responsive in unantici-
pated ways because of his experience with the other. Unlike
Remus and the little white boy, John and Uncle Julius are each
performer and audience; they engage in a variation of call-
and-response. (40)

Chesnutt further enacts this dialectic of "call-and response" in his
representation of conjure.[14] John chides Uncle Julius for clinging to black
folk superstition, including conjure. John eventually learns that conjure
is more than superstition. It is more than the thematic element of Uncle
Julius's tales. Conjure is a way of explaining what remains inexplicable
according to Euro-American reason. Conjure becomes an alternative
epistemology. Conjure, which for the most part is exercised to curse
someone or something (like a grapevine), is seemingly an embellished
aspect of Uncle Julius's storytelling. As a result, rational people would
not take conjure seriously.

Yet ironically, conjure often contributes to the persuasiveness of the
tales. That is to say, most of Uncle Julius's stories end with a moral, one
that poorly hides a benefit for him. That John is often aware of Julius's
covert motives before they are realized complicates this discussion even
further. How does one persuade an audience with obviously irrational
arguments and self-serving motives?

This strategy does not always succeed for Uncle Julius, as the title
story, "The Goophered Grapevine," makes plain. Animatedly explaining to his employer that a certain grapevine "is goophered—cunju'd, be-
witched," Uncle Julius fails to dissuade John from purchasing it. But there
are times when Julius succeeds, even when his stories suggest no traditionally logical reason why. Uncle Julius wins more than things for himself,
like sole access to a tree full of honey in "The Gray Wolf's Ha'nt" or John's
breakfast ham in "Dave's Neckliss"; he wins a hearing for conjure. In "Sis'
Becky's Pickaninny," John scoffs at the power Uncle Julius accords to a
rabbit's foot. To John's surprise, his wife eventually embraces this superstition, acquiring a rabbit's foot for herself. She turns to this charm to
aid her where medical science and a change in climate had failed.

This is not to say that Uncle Julius persuaded John or his wife to replace their Western rationalism with folk traditions or, for that matter,
to accord those perspectives with equal station. Instead, conjure as an

instance of folk superstition becomes a way of constructing (and, for Julius, momentarily controlling) reality.[15]

In the same way, AAVE, assumed inferior to standardized American English by John and his creator Chesnutt, became a way of communicating reality. AAVE frames the tales—and conjure as an element of those tales—just as standardized American English frames black dialect. Or to rephrase, Chesnutt believes that African American language, narrative, and folk culture are circumscribed by mainstream discourse. But in the process of confining this "sub"-discourse, the borders of mainstream discourse too are altered.

Julius, his tales, and dialect receive a hearing. Granted, Chesnutt neither styles Julius's wit "superior" nor accords it full equality with John's, but he does ascribe a literary value to vernacular tales that neither Joel Chandler Harris nor Thomas Nelson Page afforded them. First of all, Chesnutt lauds the intelligence of the black artist who crafts the folk tale. What is more, through conjure itself, Chesnutt provides a glimpse into the alternative epistemologies potentially evoked by black folk culture. The glimpse Chesnutt provides is narrow; the knowledge itself is limited and unrealized; nonetheless, he offers the glimpse.

Despite Chesnutt's insistence that *The Conjure Woman* was the only collection of his writings that did not address "the problems of people with mixed blood," Uncle Julius's ancestry is salient (rpt. in Gibson 126).[16] John's initial description of Uncle Julius in "The Goophered Grapevine" is worth citing in full:

> While he had been standing, I had observed he was a tall man, and though slightly bowed by the weight of years, apparently quite vigorous. He was *not entirely black,* and this fact, together with the quality of his hair, which was about six inches long and bushy, except on the top of his head, where he was quite bald, suggested a slight strain of other than negro blood. There was a shrewdness to his eyes, too, which was not altogether African, and which, as we afterwards learned from experience, was indicative of a corresponding shrewdness in his character. (*Conjure* 34, emphasis added)

Here Chesnutt capitalizes on two race myths: (1) the link between physical traits and abstract qualities and (2) the belief that any intelli-

gence blacks display evinces white ancestry. Once again, notwithstanding Chesnutt's Eurocentrism and elitism, he covertly critiques these myths.
Perhaps Julius's "slight strain of other than negro blood" sets the stage
for the import John (Chesnutt) would later accord the conjure tales. In
the same way, the first story in Chesnutt's first collection of short stories, "The Goophered Grapevine," opens up a space for Chesnutt to
discuss mixed race in subsequent writings.

Chesnutt radically revised America's race binary and introduced a
tame but equally important cutting-edge use of black dialect. His positing of mixed race as an alternative category was not new historically.
But his consideration of mixed race within the artistic arena suggests
critical implications for rhetoric and authorship.

He destabilized what the majority of the Americans of his time assumed to be the fixed, physical determinants of "blackness." And by so
doing, he further unsettled the more abstract assumption that the "black"
soul could be expressed. Even his restrictive take on black dialect was
comprehensive enough to challenge the popular belief that racial essence
was reproducible via print.

In destabilizing accepted racial categories, however, Chesnutt fixed
another: mixed race. In one sense, he did not completely reject the former
boundaries; he merely restricted the application of the designation "Negro," "colored" or "black." Chesnutt had the same investment in the
mixed-race category that others of his time had in the black and white
racial categories. For all that Chesnutt's theory on race intimates about
the power of choosing one's identity, it still fails to capture or to describe
the fluid and shifting nature of racial designations.

4

Of Color and Culture: Du Bois's Evolving Perspectives on Race

WITH REGARD TO HOW RACIAL IDENTITY SHOULD be defined, Charles Chesnutt's certainty surpassed that of his younger, formally educated friend, W. E. B. Du Bois. I partly question Chesnutt's certainty, while I remain struck by Du Bois's evolving perspectives on race. Throughout his life, Du Bois affirms—through dozens of articles, essays, and several books—particular constructions of race, only to subvert them later. This process of affirming and subverting racial designations constitutes another essential component in rethinking racialized voice. In other words, an alternative paradigm of racialized voice must be open to the flexibility represented in Du Bois's shifting takes on racial designations.

Additionally, Kwame Anthony Appiah argues that Du Bois recognized but came short of adopting the word *civilization* as a more fitting descriptor of group identity than race. Given Appiah's contention and my own interest in black folk culture, I must also explore how Du Bois's understanding of American culture generally and African American culture specifically correlates with his evolving racial ideologies. Therefore, I will examine selected writings by Du Bois from two vistas: what they say about race and what they say about culture in relation to race.

An artist, historian, and sociologist, Du Bois was conversant in myriad approaches to analyzing the race question. Arnold Rampersad observes that Du Bois's personal complexity befits the complexities of this question:

The task of understanding Du Bois is not easy. As I pointed out in 1976, he was a mass of paradoxes, "a product of black and white, poverty and privilege, love and hate. He was of New England and the South, an alien and an American, a provincial and a cosmopolite, nationalist and communist, Victorian and modern. With the soul of a poet and the intellect of a scientist, he lived at least a double life, continually compelled to the challenge of reconciling opposites." (vii)

William Edward Burghardt Du Bois was among the first persons of African descent to comprehensively address the "Negro question." From the search for black consciousness in the classic *Souls of Black Folk* to the retelling of his own experiences with the problems of the color line in his first autobiography proper *Dusk of Dawn*, Du Bois's public voice represents a prodigious effort to honor African Americans.[1]

Indeed, this tension between the public and private Du Bois functions as the crowning paradox of his career. He elevated, for example, his personal experience with racism to representative status with *Dusk of Dawn: An Essay Toward an Autobiography of the Race Concept.* Like Frederick Douglass and Charles Chesnutt (both of whom Du Bois admired), Du Bois exemplifies the problem of one black person presuming, or being presumed, to speak for the race.

Revising Race: Personal Odyssey and Public Revelation

One aspect of Du Bois's ever-changing takes on race is the movement of intratextual revision within his writings. By "intratextuality" I mean the dialogue, the overt or covert rhetorical interchanges that occur between two or more writings by the same author. An intratextual analysis of Du Bois's work will foster, to some extent, the type of questioning, critique, and reformulating one would expect to find from an intertextual analysis of works by two authors.

One example of this process emerges in Du Bois's account of his upbringing in Great Barrington, Massachusetts, and his initial encounter with the South. Du Bois was born in Great Barrington in 1868. Although he was not to witness firsthand the harsh racism southern blacks experienced until he attended college and taught in the South, he always recognized himself as black. Never mind that his complexion was a clue to his partial white ancestry. He was—as the one-drop rule of his time dictated—black.

Still, an optimism marked Du Bois's childhood. Du Bois says of Great Barrington in *Dusk of Dawn,* "The color line was manifest and yet not absolutely drawn." To illustrate this point, Du Bois provides a telling incident about a cousin who brought home a white wife. Surprisingly, the only two objections Du Bois's family raised were that this cousin did not have enough money to support a wife nor did they know anything about this woman's background.

More important, in *The Autobiography of W. E. B. Du Bois,* published some twenty years after *Dusk of Dawn,* this optimism about his boyhood does not change substantially. Certainly, Du Bois recalls instances of overt racism. Entering high school, for example, Du Bois "began to feel the pressure of the 'veil of color'; in little matters at first and then in larger" (83). Yet the young William (or "Willie" as David Levering Lewis reminds us Du Bois was called [W. E. B.]) held fast to the belief that the Protestant work ethic would enable one to transcend the color line. From his mother he acquired an almost unwavering trust in this essential facet of the American Dream:

> The secret of life and the loosing of the color bar, then, lay
> in excellence, in accomplishment. If others of my family, of
> my colored kin, had stayed in school instead of quitting early
> for small jobs, they could have risen to equal whites. On this
> my mother quietly insisted. There was no real discrimination
> on account of color—it was all a matter of hard work. (75)

Although Du Bois's awareness of discrimination increased significantly in the South, he clung for several years to the naive hope that excellence would ultimately eliminate racial distinctions. This is one of the reasons why classical education was an integral part of his racial uplift strategy. Social equality would follow the manifestation of intellectual equality.

At seventeen, Du Bois left Great Barrington to attend Fisk University in Nashville, Tennessee, and understandably, his perception of race and racism were radically transformed. In a sense, there were positive and negative edges to Du Bois's full acceptance of his black racial identity upon arriving in the South. Being black was not incidental, as it theoretically had been in the North.

A lesser but still important influence on Du Bois's firm identification with blackness was the various complexions of African Americans represented at Fisk—he particularly noticed the women. Of course, this reverie may reveal as much about Du Bois's heightening romantic interest as it does about his emerging sense of racial identity. Suffice it to say that a more essential message arises: a variety of physical appearances and differing social conditions are captured under the umbrella of blackness:

> I was thrilled to be for the first time among so many people of my own color or rather of such various and such extraordinary colors, which I had only glimpsed before, but who it seemed were bound to me by new and exciting eternal ties. . . . So I came to a region where the world was split into white and black halves, and where the darker half was held back by race prejudice and legal bounds, as well as by deep ignorance and dire poverty. But facing this was not a lost group, but at Fisk a microcosm of a world and a civilization in potentiality. Into this world I leapt with enthusiasm. A new loyalty and allegiance replaced my Americanism: henceforward I was a Negro. (*Autobiography* 107–8)

Two principal factors, then, contributed to Du Bois's initial, conscious adoption of black identity: the kaleidoscope of "colored" complexions he became aware of at Fisk and the harsher, more overt racism of the South. Both show how blackness is constructed existentially, socially, and geographically. Neither factor, at this early moment in Du Bois's life, allowed him to fully grasp something other than the one-drop rule to measure racial identity. Some of the women at Fisk "looked white," but Du Bois classifies them as "Negro." The more intriguing problem for Du Bois, and for many other thinkers of that time, was that black identity was primarily defined by racism.

Unfortunately, *The Autobiography* contains examples of Du Bois slipping into the nineteenth-century racist generalizations that he would later decry. During his studies at his high school in Great Barrington, one other black person attended. Du Bois "was very much ashamed of" this "dark boy" "because he did not excel the whites" as Du Bois did. Doubtless, Du Bois feared that any mediocrity on the part of this classmate would confirm the whites' assumptions about the innate stupidity of all blacks.

But in entertaining this thought, Du Bois showed his tacit acceptance of racist views regarding the nexus between color and character.

Be that as it may, Du Bois left Fisk with a solid sense of his own identity as a black intact. He entered Harvard University by his own admission "as a Negro, not simply by birth, but recognizing myself as a member of a segregated caste whose situation I accepted but was determined to work from within the caste to find my way out" (*Autobiography* 132).

Hence, even before Du Bois began to officially undertake his polemical exposition of the race question, he broached the impasse between race as a biological reality and race as a social construct. Moreover, he possessed a burgeoning sensibility to the limitations of theoretical knowledge in solving the race problem, and he made a noticeable move toward political activism.

Before detailing Du Bois's public exposition of his evolving race ideologies, I now preview this progression outright: Du Bois moves from constructing race "biologically" to constructing it "sociohistorically" and just short of constructing it "culturally."[2] This progression begins with "The Conservation of Races," a paper Du Bois delivered in 1897, a date that also marked the inception of the American Negro Academy:[3]

> What, then, is a race? It is generally a vast family of human beings, generally of common blood, and language, always of common history, traditions and impulses, who are both voluntarily and involuntarily striving together for the accomplishment of certain more or less vividly conceived ideals of life. (817)

In the earliest stages of his career, Du Bois questioned tentatively the logic of accepting shared physical traits as unequivocal determinants of race. The phrase "generally of common blood" validates my use of "tentatively."

Du Bois did not dismiss totally, however, the idea that race could be analyzed from a scientific standpoint. His continental education produced in him the same blind trust in science that others of his background possessed. He attended Harvard and the University of Berlin when pseudoscientific racism was increasing in popularity. In fact, one of his professors at Berlin, Heinrich von Treitschke, declared during a lecture that "[m]ulattos are inferior; they feel themselves inferior" (*Autobiography* 165).

Consequently, as I discuss Du Bois's shift from so-called scientific to sociohistorical conceptions of race, I am not contending for either a swift or total transition. Du Bois never came to dismiss the overarching notion of race itself or the practice of classifying people by common physical traits. He only expands the racial categories from three to eight (Appiah, "Uncompleted" 23).

Du Bois's employment of *impulses* is also problematical. Its use leaves the impression that despite what Du Bois might say to the contrary, nineteenth-century researchers would be partly justified in ascribing a "common history and traditions" to "a common biology" ("Uncompleted" 25–26). Moreover, *common history* and *traditions* constrict his enterprise. The words fail to take into account Du Bois's ethnically mixed heritage.

By the time Du Bois pens his autobiography, *Dusk of Dawn,* he is prepared to repudiate race as "a scientific concept" ("Uncompleted" 32). Du Bois was most polemical in this claim. "Thus it is easy to see that scientific definition of race is impossible; it is easy to prove that physical characteristics are not so inherited as to make it possible to divide the world into races" (*Dusk* 654).

The book's subtitle, *An Essay Toward an Autobiography of a Race Concept,* intimates the stages in Du Bois's understanding of race in at least two major ways: one as the subject who has experientially arrived at a profounder understanding of race, and the other as a writer who must reconstruct and communicate the events leading to his epiphany as subject. Without discounting the phenomenal strides Du Bois made in terms of his own understanding of racialization, he still could not free himself from employing race or some comparable euphemism to essentialize "his" people. Or as Appiah remarks,

> Even in the passage that follows Du Bois's explicit disavowal of the scientific concept of race, the reference to "common history," "the one long memory," "the social heritage and slavery,"—only lead us back into the now familiar move of substituting a sociohistorical conception of race for a biological one; but that is simply to bury the biological conception below the surface, not to transcend it. ("Uncompleted" 34)

The various euphemisms Du Bois employed, so contends Appiah, did little to transcend or, better yet, disrupt the race construct. On the whole, the pieces I have considered evoke a continuum of defining, revising, and deferring what informs both the idea of race as well as any attempt to dismantle its authority.

Du Bois also moves toward dismantling the authority of race by broadening the term *colored* to include nonwhite peoples of other cultures. He makes this empowering move both in *Dark Princess* (published in 1928) and *Dusk of Dawn*. This move was empowering for American blacks because it broadened the scope of their struggle from a national to international scale. Likewise, universalizing "coloredness" predates Du Bois's full-fledged Pan-Africanism, a doctrine that would later find advocates like Malcolm X. In fact, as early as 1915, Du Bois had been fascinated with the idea of nonwhite races of the world revolting against the white race.[4]

But there is more at stake in broadening the term *colored* than political empowerment. Du Bois blurred the borders of one of the most common words for characterizing African Americans during that period. Like *black, colored* carries with it a number of negative connotations. The colored man's life is *colored,* marked by duplicity.

Consequently, Du Bois sought in books such as *Dark Princess* to blur the borders of "colored" identity. Through his light-skinned black protagonist Matthew Townes, Du Bois simultaneously critiques and reveres the one-drop rule. To an Arab who observed that Townes was not dark-skinned, he retorts, "Black blood with us in America is a matter of spirit not simply of flesh" (19). When Kautilya, daughter of an Indian maharajah comes to America, she is deemed "colored" by those who take her for an African American, a mistake Townes had made upon seeing her for the first time.

Alexander Crummell and the Formation of Black Cultural Elitism

To appreciate Du Bois's complex stance on black folk culture, as well as how this stance informed and was informed by his conceptions of race, one must know something about Du Bois's most influential black mentor, Alexander Crummell. Even a review of Crummell's life will illustrate his influence on Du Bois's ideas about race and culture.

Born in New York in 1819, Crummell was an Episcopal minister and major civil rights advocate. Ten years before Du Bois's birth and until 1872, he lived in Liberia, working as a missionary. A graduate of Cambridge and founder of the American Negro Academy in 1897, Crummell produced a number of works on Pan-Africanism, nationalism, and protest. Part of his reason for founding the American Negro Academy was to contest Booker T. Washington's accommodationist policies.

Du Bois borrowed a degree of his obsession with European classical education, Pan-Africanism, protest, and art as propaganda from Crummell. But Du Bois also adopted Crummell's distaste for the emotionalism that often accompanied religious practices in black rural communities, "the 'get happy' philosophy of 'feel good religion'" (Moses 5). Unlike Du Bois, Crummell was not an agnostic, yet both deemed the emotionalism displayed in some southern black churches to be histrionic and primitive.

Crummell engaged in what Wilson J. Moses calls "racial chauvinism," specifically "in his characterizations of various African peoples" and his "hostility toward mulattos." This attitude was decidedly ironic, given Crummell's passion for Pan-Africanism and deep admiration for Du Bois.[5]

Crummell's initial contact with the classics came through a segregated school in New York. Thus, before Crummell was aware that whites could master the classics, he knew that other blacks could. Like Crummell, then, Du Bois struggled to reconcile what he considered the honorable yet primitive spirit of black folk culture with European high culture. Neither Crummell's nor Du Bois's respective philosophies privileged black folk culture as they did European culture. African American artistic culture, such as it was, had a long way to go before it could measure up to European high culture. Addressing society's need to recognize blacks as more than laborers, Crummell clarifies this progression:

> What he needs is Civilization. He needs the increase of his higher wants, of his mental and spiritual needs. *This,* mere animal labor has never given him, and never can give him. But it will come to him, as an individual, and as a class, just in proportion as the higher culture comes to his leaders and teachers, and so gets into his schools, academies and colleges; and then enters his pulpits; and so filters down into his families and his homes; and the Negro learns he is no longer a serf. . . . But when his culture fits him for something more than a field hand or mechanic, he is to have an open door set wide

before him! And that culture, according to his capacity, he
must claim as his rightful heritage, as a man; —not stinted
training, not caste education, *not a Negro curriculum.* (297,
emphasis added)

Crummell moves his white audience beyond the assumptions regarding
the intellectual limitations of African Americans. That blacks are capable
of mastering the classics, should be afforded the chance to do so, and
should receive the honors that accompany having done so are proposi-
tions worthy of Crummell's most vigorous argument.

But why does learning European classics necessarily represent "higher
wants" or "spiritual needs"? In one sense, it could be argued that great
literature, regardless of the race or class from which it originates, belongs
to all people. But comparing the black person's learning European high
culture to "claiming his rightful culture as a man" reveals the Eurocen-
trisim that informs Crummell's argument. Moreover, the passage implies
that no "Negro curriculum" is truly a part of the American heritage.

I wonder to what extent, then, both Crummell and Du Bois curtail
their efforts to demonstrate that blacks are capable of achieving intellectually on par with whites. To what degree does Du Bois's scientific
training cause him to hold on to residues of the race essentialism of the
nineteenth century? The Eurocentrism Crummell passed on to Du Bois
restricted Du Bois's from completely transcending race.

Soul and Substance: Du Bois's Divided Stance on Black Folk Culture

Unquestionably, certain aspects of African American folk culture, particularly the spirituals, viscerally moved Du Bois. Du Bois structures his
master treatise, *The Souls of Black Folk,* around epigraphs that align lines
from European poetry with blank bars of music, signifying lines from the
spirituals. Du Bois uses these epigraphs, along with the last chapter, entitled "The Sorrow Songs," to emphasize the internal tenacity, raw courage, and American spirit mirrored in the spirituals. The last chapter also
adds words to blank bars of music, thus forming a textual climax.

Beginning in *Souls,* the spirituals or "sorrow songs" became for Du
Bois the principal motif of African American culture, not to mention the
quintessential case study of what this developing culture could offer
larger American culture. Of all the aspects of black folk culture that Du

Bois belittles in *The Quest of the Silver Fleece,* for example, the power of song is revered.

Further, concerning black dialect, both Keith Byerman and Arnold Rampersad concede its apparent absence from Du Bois's writing, *The Quest of the Silver Fleece* being no exception. In that novel, Du Bois writes about one of the protagonists dropping "Negro dialect"; however, he never illuminates for his readers, even through orthographic distortions, the speech patterns of that dialect.

Cornel West admires Du Bois's immense contribution to African American thought and culture. Similar to Byerman, however, West believes that Du Bois's Victorianism and unfailing trust in Enlightenment reason limited his appreciation of black folk culture: "Du Bois was first and foremost a black New England Victorian seduced by the Enlightenment ethos and enchanted with the American Dream" (Gates and West 57). West criticizes Du Bois for his inability to relate to and, as a result, articulate a realistic vision for the black masses. By Du Bois's own admission, his extensive education distanced him from most whites of the time. Other scholars, such as the late historian Nathan I. Huggins, have observed that many of Du Bois's African American contemporaries considered him aloof. Since, so West's argument goes, Victorianism and the "Enlightenment ethos" were ideologies that systematically denied the intelligence of blacks in general, Du Bois, as a proponent of these ideologies, was restricted from complete identification with black folk culture.

Granted, Du Bois was indeed limited by his Eurocentrism. Even so, he was not trying to transform blacks into darker whites. Instead, through the Talented Tenth's facility with the classics, along with the cultivation of what he believed to be the nobler elements of black folk culture and character, blacks could prove themselves to whites. Du Bois neither expected nor desired every African American to pursue higher learning. Some would; some would not. But all could show themselves worthy of democracy.

Yet this larger effort to have blacks prove themselves is the core problem. It represents the same fallacy James Weldon Johnson appropriated about dialect. That is to say, Du Bois reinforced inadvertently the myth that something was wrong with blacks innately. Proving oneself as an individual is one thing, proving oneself as a representative of a group, another. Du Bois should have known better. Against his better judgment, he led a campaign to aggressively recruit African Americans to serve during World War I, with the confidence that their heroism would win them the human rights they deserved.[6]

This did not happen. As David Levering Lewis notes, discrimination against blacks actually intensified after the war, in many instances, directly against black veterans *(When)*. Likewise, the competence and visibility of Du Bois's colleagues, the Talented Tenth, did not persuade the white masses to acknowledge the intelligence or humanity of blacks, even though there were many Ivy League graduates (like Du Bois) among the group.

Once again, this aspect of Du Bois's project was destined to fail because it is a catch-22 for a group of despised people to prove themselves as a race. Such thinking further conflicts with the basic assumption of the Protestant work ethic and of the American Dream—individual merit. With blacks, any instance of ignorance or unruly behavior was, and often is, perceived by whites as common, while obviously well mannered and brilliant blacks are aberrations.

Overall, then, Cornel West may be right in asserting that Du Bois so deified European high culture that his mind was not open enough to the unique value of black folk culture. But West's analysis could have included a discussion of reason and spirit in *The Souls of Black Folk* that, like Du Bois's other public works, speaks to a personal struggle. The fact that Du Bois ends up in Ghana has a great deal to say about the respect for African culture, as well as the hopelessness regarding American culture, at which he eventually arrives.

For most of his life, Du Bois saw black folk culture as the soul of America largely because it had become a part of his soul. As I suggested earlier in this chapter, Du Bois realized this connection at Fisk, but he received his initiation before going to the South. After receiving the news that he would attend Fisk, Du Bois recalls the first time he heard "Negro folk songs." It was in a Congregational Church of his northern hometown. Through this experience he claimed "to recognize something inherently and deeply my own" *(Dusk* 570).

The notion of soul kept Du Bois's continental snobbishness from totally choking off his interest in African American folk culture. By "soul," Du Bois means "the consciousness of a people," borrowing a Germanic concept.[7] Similarly, he uses "folk" in the Germanic sense of "nation" (Zamir). But it may have been this passion to develop a racial-national consciousness, based on his own cultural consciousness, that also inhibited Du Bois from completely transcending the race construct.

As Du Bois's limited view of culture restricted his evolving view of race, his aesthetic perceptions became racially imbued. In "Criteria of Negro Art," he makes a statement that is worth citing in full:

> Thus it is the bounden duty of black America to begin this great work of the creation of Beauty, of the preservation of Beauty, of the realization of Beauty, and we must use in this work all the methods that men have used before. And what have been the tools of the artist in times gone by? First of all, he has used the Truth—not for the sake of truth, not as a scientist seeking truth, but as one upon whom Truth eternally thrust itself as the highest handmaid of the imagination, as the one great vehicle of universal understanding. Again artists have used Goodness—goodness in all its aspects of justice, honor and right—not for the sake of ethical sanction but as the one true method for gaining sympathy. . . . Thus all art is propaganda and ever must be, despite the wailing of the purists. I stand in utter shamelessness and say that whatever art I have for writing has been used always for gaining the right of black folk to love and enjoy. ("Criteria" 1000)

This passage recalls Du Bois's dual role during the Harlem Renaissance. He was more than a race leader, a title he had acquired shortly after Booker T. Washington's death. Du Bois had also become the secretary of the NAACP and editor of the *Crisis* magazine, sponsored by the NAACP. The position with the *Crisis* presented the Ivy League and German-educated scholar with one of his greatest challenges—he became the arbiter of fine black writing. This was an unlikely position for a man who did not consider himself a good writer. And since Du Bois belonged to what Robert Hemenway considers the first generation of Harlem intellectuals (38–39), his criteria for art were primarily political. This is not to say that Du Bois did not flirt with art for art's sake.

Du Bois infuses the above passage with the aura of divine authority. He accomplishes this in part by capitalizing *Truth, Beauty,* and *Goodness*—as he does *Art* (the synonym of *Beauty*) and *Justice* (contained in a part of the passage not quoted). One could counter by noting that he styles "Truth the handmaid of the imagination," hence subordinating it to Art. Conjoined with Art and Goodness or Beauty and Justice, however, Truth is deified, as it becomes a manifestation of what amounts to a sacred, artistic creed.

He further projects the guise of maintaining objectivity, swiftly and smoothly moving from third to first person by the end of the passage. Even his references to his disenfranchised brethren are described in quasi-detached language: notice "the duty of black America" and "the right of black folk."

In short, Du Bois's Eurocentric perception of African American folk culture actually restricted his ability to define larger African American culture and identity. Still, his incessant desire to find a more fitting descriptor for race is worthy of any writer's unceasing reflection.

Occupying the space between a proper reverence for folk elements of African American culture and a healthy skepticism about fixed race designations is a formidable task, as Chesnutt's and Du Bois's noteworthy efforts indicate. Zora Neale Hurston came remarkably close to occupying this middle space.

5

"Reading My Words but Not My Mind": Hurston's Ironic Voice

ZORA NEALE HURSTON SHOULD BE INCLUDED IN any critical discussion of black voice. Like Chesnutt and Du Bois, she affirmed the value of African American folk culture. Unlike either of them, she did so without implying any underlying inferiority of that culture. Like her older colleagues, she contested traditional ideas about race, but she did so as an individual, without presuming to define racial identity for anyone else. Of greatest significance, her career and writings draw attention to some of the points at which gender, race, and writing converge. From her life, writers of color can derive approaches to engaging the question, to what extent do race and gender control the individual's construction of authorial ethos?

Hurston defies simple characterization. Extremely proud of the traditions of the all-black town in which she was raised, she was accused by many black artists of being a "happy darkie" and of denigrating her people. She studied anthropology with the renowned Franz Boas but remained intrigued with the mystical world of voodoo. And through her ethnographic masterpiece *Mules and Men,* she blurred the lines among genres: can social scientific writing also be artistic?

She set the standard for the inclusion of folklore and vernacular in fiction. Many of her works describe the blessings and perils of marriage, yet she was anything but conventional in her view of this institution, her attitudes most resembling those of Janie Crawford, the heroine in *Their Eyes Were Watching God*. In short, Hurston's life and work are subject to many interpretations.

According to Mary Helen Washington, reports of Hurston's physical appearance can function curiously as a "paradigm" for her intellectual complexity. Washington's essay conveys three dramatically different descriptions of Hurston's complexion:

> Whether Zora Neale Hurston was black as coal, light yellow, or light brown seems to have depended a great deal on the imagination and mind set of the observer. These three divergent descriptions of her color serve as a paradigm for the way Zora Hurston, the personality, and Zora Hurston, the writer, have been looked upon in the world which judged her. Outstanding novelist, skilled folklorist, journalist and critic, Zora Hurston was for thirty years the most prolific black woman writer in America. And yet, from what has been written about her, it would be difficult to judge the quality of her work or even to know what color she was. (7)

Washington's article, "Zora Neale Hurston: A Woman in Half Shadow," was written in the 1970s. Although the considerable increase in scholarship on Hurston since that time is attributable in large part to Washington and the more notable contributions of Alice Walker, Hurston remains a woman obscured by shadow. For Washington, this may be because of how Hurston has been perceived. But I think it has more to do with how she projected herself. From her childhood, Hurston resisted categorization and possessed "a high tolerance for contradiction."[1]

Moreover, this resistance was motivated neither by the desire to create an alternative racial identity (as it was for Chesnutt) nor to find a more fitting descriptor for race (as it was for Du Bois). Rather, Hurston's quest is rooted in play of the search itself. Her life and writings are marked by endless ambiguities, and that is precisely how she wanted it.

Wearing Race

Early in her career, Hurston accepted race as a social and personal paradox. As a result, she never sought to conclusively define her racial identity. Her 1928 essay "How It Feels to Be Colored Me" provides a most ironic critique of race. This article was published for *World Tomorrow,* "a white journal sympathetic to Harlem Renaissance writers" (B. Johnson 131). Even the title of the article evokes irony. The elimination of *like,* as in "How It Feels to Be Colored *Like* Me," intimates that what Hurston's readers construed as objective reality—her "color"—she framed as subjective experience.

Further, had Hurston used *Negro* instead of *colored,* her initial projection of blackness (and race) as variable would not have been as effective rhetorically. Barbara Johnson offers a key observation in this regard:

> [T]he essay is dotted with sentences playing complex variations on title words "feel," "color," and "me": But I am not tragically colored. I do not always feel colored. I feel most colored when I am thrown against a white background. At certain times, I have no race, I am me. I have no separate feelings about being an American citizen and colored. (133)

Johnson evidently views Hurston's title as providing the threads that form the ideological fabric for the entire essay. Further, if Hurston was addressing, as Johnson surmises, a question typically asked by liberal whites—"How does it feel to be colored?"—then the title, and seemingly the essay's content, would hardly threaten Hurston's white audience.

Hurston relegates her "color" to the province of subjectivity by showing how her racial identity was initially shaped not by her own perceptions but rather by the colored perceptions of some white people she met on a riverboat when she was a child. In effect, "becoming colored" has more to do with social interactions than with genetic characteristics. Since that is the case, Zora creates a space in which color can be understood as shifting instead of static, or to borrow from Johnson, as a matter of "seeing and wearing" (136).

One of the most striking moments in the essay occurs when Hurston recalls a time she and a white friend were listening to jazz together; she focuses on their divergent responses. She is moved to "dance wildly" and "yeeoow!" He merely "drums the table with his fingertips." Hurston concludes,

> Music. The great blobs of purple and red have not touched him. He has only heard what I felt. He is far away and I see him dimly across the ocean and the continent that have fallen

between us. He is so paled with whiteness and I am so colored. ("How" 154)

A cursory reading of this passage makes Hurston guilty of stereotypic generalizing. Whites are not moved by jazz the way that blacks are. That is, blacks have an innate tie to this music. Johnson counters this superficial reading, recommending instead one more in keeping with the ironic play manifested elsewhere in the essay. The colors employed to describe black feelings are "skin paint," not "skin complexion." Thus "the 'tonal veil' is rent indeed, on the level at once of color, of sound, and of literary style" (B. Johnson 134). Further, the white man's "drumming with his fingers" is an "alienated synecdoche for bodily release," supposedly associated with the jungle.

The images of the paint and veil have another significance. One often speaks of emotions in terms of color. Consider "feeling blue" or "being green with envy," for example. Such descriptions are immediately recognized as figurative. Including something as essentially colorless as emotions gives Hurston's readers the opportunity to question whether racial color can be taken objectively.

With the veil, Hurston adapts a critical image in African American thought. Du Bois used "the veil" to describe the insurmountable differences between blacks and whites. They are, as Hurston says, "oceans" and "continents" apart, even while sitting next to each other. Again, Hurston complicates the impenetrable differences between blacks and whites that Du Bois assumes.

"How It Feels to Be Colored Me" is a satirical masterpiece. Hurston projects an ethos that is fervently embraced by her audience. While their arms are open, however, she comes in for the kill. She persuades her white audience to appropriate an alternative notion of blackness before they can say "Nigger."

In "Art and Such," Hurston discusses the fallacy of blacks allowing slavery to influence their collective identity. She feels that some blacks enact this thinking by revering and, consequently, holding to the title "Race Leader," along with other antiquated trappings from the post-Reconstruction period:

In the very face of a situation as different from the 1880s as chalk is from cheese, they stand around and mouth the same trite phrases, and try their practiced-best to look sad. They call spirituals "Our Sorrow Songs" and other such tomfoolery in an effort to get into the spotlight if possible without having ever done anything to improve education, industry, invention, art, and never having uttered a quotable line. Though he is being jostled about these days and paid scant attention, the Race Man is still with us—he and his Reconstruction pullings. His job today is to rush around seeking for something he can resent. (23)

This scathing critique appears to deprecate the contributions of black leaders during Hurston's time. Given the degree of racism that prevailed during 1938 when this essay was written, Hurston's remark might strike current readers as especially egregious. I do not believe Hurston either intended to downplay generally black leaders' contributions or justify racism.

Certainly, she ostensibly honors the forefathers whom these contemporary race men claim to follow. She makes a passing reference to the greatness of Frederick Douglass, but perhaps only as a concession to those new "Race Leaders" who were sure to have greater doubts about her loyalty to the cause had she failed to do so. On the other hand, the allusion to Douglass might be judicious in another way. Although Douglass was a "Race Leader" during his younger years, revisions of his autobiography suggest that he was becoming less of a race man, opting rather to be known simply as an American.[2]

Whatever the case, Hurston introduces an important idea in the above passage: the progress of African Americans can be neither defined nor confined to one period, a period which Hurston sees as transitional at best. Furthermore, partly in this passage, partly elsewhere in the essay, Hurston describes the conflicting agendas of these "Race Men."

Specifically, they wanted to hold on to their heritage as slaves, while creating black colleges that replicated white colleges (22–23). On one level, then, Hurston faults these men for attempting to occupy two spaces at once in order to create a new space for their race. The problem is that this "new" space is more restrictive than the former spaces depicted in slavery (heritage) and segregation (all white colleges), especially as the new space prescribes and proscribes the function of black literature and the role of the black writer:

> Can the black poet sing a song to the morning? Up springs
> the song to his lips but it is fought back. He says to himself,
> "Ah this is a beautiful song inside of me. I feel the morning
> in my throat, I will sing of the star and the morning." Then
> his background thrusts itself between his lips and the star
> mutters, "Ought I not to be singing of our sorrows? This is
> what is expected of me and I shall be considered forgetful of
> our past and present. If I do not some will even call me a
> coward. The one subject for a Negro is the Race and its suf-
> ferings and so the song of morning must be choked back. I
> will write of lynching instead." ("Art" 23–24)

Hurston characterizes the desire to "sing a song to the morning" as
a creative impulse. The thought of "the race and its sufferings," conversely, "thrusts itself between" the black writer's "lips," thus reflecting external artistic restrictions. The former inclination speaks to the
personal longing to capture one's creative vision, the latter to an imposed
duty to submit to the expectations of one's ethnic group. Hurston believes that the interchanging of the individual's aesthetic with the group's
sociopolitical agenda limits the black writer's particular enterprise.

Hurston quickly adds, "It is not to be concluded from these meager
offerings in the arts that Negro talent is lacking" (26). Indeed, she styles
the "Art Wars" among African Americans as regional, according the
status of "genuine artist" anonymously to herself and explicitly to James
Weldon Johnson, both from Florida. It could be that she mentions Johnson's *The Autobiography of an Ex-Coloured Man,* which is about passing, to once more expose the essential arbitrariness of linking political
takes on race to writing.

As I alluded earlier, other African American writers accused Hurston
of trivializing the way blacks were oppressed. Richard Wright and Sterling Brown, for instance, chided Hurston for not vividly depicting the
horrors of the South in her writing. However, to some extent, those who
claim that Hurston never spoke out against racism are ignoring much
of her work. In fact, many of her statements against racism were at once
overt and unconventional. For example, Hurston objected to the 1954
Brown v. the Board of Education desegregation ruling because she believed that the decision implied the inferiority of black teachers.[3] Her

valid objection and honorable intentions were dismantled by her controversial stance.

Perhaps Hurston's most unconventional and controversial critiques of race, though, are found in sections of her autobiography, *Dust Tracks on the Road*. In one such episode, Hurston recalls when, as a child, she developed a friendship with a highly respected white man from a neighboring town, with whom her parents occasionally allowed her to go fishing. While conversing during one such outing, the white man encouraged Zora not to grow up to be a "Nigger."

The rub is that Hurston does not acknowledge the term as pejorative against blacks exclusively. On the contrary, she goes out of her way to explain how this term is totally devoid of racial import, having more to do with vices common to people of all races. Of course, anyone could dispute Hurston's observation. "Nigger" was and is employed to disparage blacks. This episode, among others, caused Sterling Brown to object fiercely to the book. Understandably, then, Brown saw Hurston as someone who revered whites and chose to ignore their racism at any cost.

I am not denying the essential validity of Brown's objections. For my purpose, however, I am concerned less with what Hurston does in this instance than why. Maybe she preempts feminist and postcolonial theorists in arguing that oppressed people have the power to revise or reject designations from the hegemony: they can name themselves. This strategy was likewise employed during the 1960s when African Americans started using the designation "black," also once deemed derogatory, as an honorable one. Rap groups such as NWA (Niggas with Attitudes) and BWA (Bitches with Attitudes) have made similar decisions. Although, as Michael Eric Dyson, among others, has effectively argued, there is a decided difference, phonologically and orthographically, between hip-hop culture's use of *Nigga* and American culture's use of *Nigger*.

Nevertheless, Hurston attempts to clarify that the racist characteristics some whites believed inherent in blackness were transracial: hence, some whites are "Niggers" too. I am contending neither that this term be used now nor that Hurston should have used it then. Yet her gesture speaks to the argument that fixed formulations of race and racism could be unfixed.

Hurston takes another unconventional stance in the "My People, My People" section of her autobiography. The title of this chapter reflects an expression blacks have used among themselves to criticize undesirable behavior in other blacks. Specifically, this type of criticism involves generalizing about blacks that would be deemed racist if a white person were to do it.

Hurston sagaciously points out, however, examples not only of misbehaving on the part of blacks but of their qualities as well. This move is an important one because representatives of the "Talented Tenth," such as Du Bois and Locke, often believed that blacks should not write about uneducated or unruly blacks. By so doing, they might perpetuate for white readers the image of African American inferiority.

Hurston saw the fallacy in the Talented Tenth's plan to supplant the negative propaganda white writers produced against blacks with their own exclusively positive propaganda.[4] To expose only the *best* side of African American experience privileges white society's definition of "best." But more important, Hurston's enterprise in "My People, My People" afforded her another chance to complicate race and, possibly, to censure whites.

Some of Hurston's critiques of racism were a little more conventional. "What White Publishers Won't Print," written in 1950, surpasses earlier essays in projecting an embittered tone. Much of this may be attributable to the time. The piece was composed two years after Hurston was wrongly accused of child molestation, a charge that was literally celebrated in the black press. Perhaps Hurston had an ax to grind with whites as well as blacks. Irrespective of what her ulterior motives might have been, she continues her veiled critique of race as static reality. The project of this essay is direct: white publishers could but do not publish stories about blacks that underscore the common humanity that they share with whites. She adds that this need often goes unmet by some black writers as well:

> The blank is NOT filled by the fiction built around upper class Negroes exploiting the race problem. Rather, it tends to point up. A college-bred Negro still is not a person like other folks, but an interesting problem, more or less. (169)

She continues, as in "Art and Such," to show how the obsession with racial injustice might foil artistic purposes, actually subverting what black writers claimed they were promoting. Contrasting her "art for art's sake" aesthetic with the more common "art as propaganda" approach posited by many of the first-generation Harlem intellectuals, Hurston remarks,

> Outside of racial attitudes, there is still another reason why this literature should exist. Literature and other arts are supposed to hold up the mirror to nature. With only the fractional "exceptional" and "quaint" portrayed, a true picture of Negro life cannot be. A great principle of national art has been violated. (173)

Although I consider this passage yet another example of Hurston's rhetorical acumen, I wonder whether she has fallen into an inverted version of the trap into which she envisions other black writers falling. That is to say, they mask their social agenda under the guise of art. Is she masking an artistic agenda under the guise of human equality? My reading is also questionable, for it implies that Hurston had little interest in social issues. And as I have already indicated, that was not the case. Hurston was a complex person and, often, a satirical and playful writer. One may not conclude from these facts, however, that an essay like this one was deliberately duplicitous.

All of the essays discussed thus far are astonishing in that with them, Hurston simultaneously embraces and, to some degree, steps outside the race construct. These essays are and are not about color. Reading "What White Publishers Won't Print," for example, as an unambiguous critique of white publishers failing to regard the totality of black life is to miss a profounder subtext, one that if played out, could dismantle the authority of race and disrupt the hierarchy presented in the text proper. In other words, "wearing race" complements race as a way of reading as I explicated in chapter 2. Both metaphors speak to the personal, social, political, and aesthetic flexibility a more mobile construction of racialized voice would allow.

Flirting with Feminism: From Deifying to Defying Traditional Roles

Like her construction of race, Hurston's public presentation of gender came from a personal place. Also, as with race, Hurston's take on gender can be found where the conventional and unconventional converge. Although she experienced two failed marriages, Hurston seemed to believe it possible to balance both the roles of spouse and artist. Among all of Hurston's black female characters, Janie Crawford most resembles Hurston's attitudes, if not actions, about love. As Robert Hemenway opines, Hurston, like Janie, had to experience the sexism in a traditional male-female relationship before her "selfhood" could evolve despite that sexism. Obviously Hurston faced sexism related to her role as author. For the male-dominated Harlem Renaissance, Hurston's facility with multiple personal stances awakened some of their envy and not so latent sexism. The same Hurston who could identify experientially with black folk culture, or passively play the "happy darkie," could also aggressively stand up for her rights as an artist. And this assertiveness challenged many male authors, including Hurston's one-time good friend Langston Hughes. Concerning the now well-known controversy that surrounded Hurston and Hughes's collaboration on the play *Mule Bone*, Hemenway concludes,

> Hughes's construction of events is subtly designed to make Zora Neale Hurston appear a fickle woman representative of her sex, nervous and moody in New Jersey, and, above all, a "funny creature." In short he represents a chauvinistic interpretation of their collaboration. (146)

The formidable gender issues Hurston faced as a female author undoubtedly account partly for her reemergence during the 1960s and 1970s. Cheryl Wall's observation that the "black consciousness and feminist movements spurred the rediscovery and reassessment of Hurston's work" becomes all the more striking, since many African American women artists viewed the Black Arts movement as male-centric. This is not to say that African American women embraced the women's liberation movement uncritically. As Paula Giddings, among others, has argued, black women distrusted "white" feminism for at least two reasons, the first being the limelight this movement often took from the fight for black civil rights and the second being the way some white feminists minimized the significance of race in sociopolitical oppression.

Still, Hurston's emerging feminism was evident in more than her encounters with sexist authors. Rather, her evolving feminism stems in part from her larger desire to reconcile formal education with informal experiences. Gwendolyn Mikell has argued that Hurston's feminist perspectives underwent a major change through her formal education and experience as an ethnographer. In fact, while she respected her professors at Howard and Columbia, no professor could get her to accept their interpretations uncritically. One of her more famous Howard professors, Alain Locke, argued that black culture was not "crudely imitative of white culture." Instead, black culture had its own "valid continuity and logic—not to mention historical depth" (Mikell 56).

Mikell goes on to note that Hurston deemed Locke's analysis rich but inadequate, as it failed to comment upon the roles of African American female intellectuals in the larger black community. Hurston found similar limitations, according to Mikell, with her anthropological training at Columbia, training that while striving to objectively examine the lives of oppressed people missed the subjective nuances of black female life in the United States and in the Caribbean. Nevertheless, since Hurston hailed from a southern rural background, she could attest to the character and strength of that location and, more to the point, of the women residing there. As a result, Hurston believed that she would receive the reconciliation she sought between education and experience as she returned to her home region and folk to perform ethnographic study.

Franz Boas: White Patriarchy and Nonwhite Cultures

In chapter 2, I discussed how Boas discredited the pseudoscientific racism of his time. He was among the first anthropologists to argue that nonwhite cultures should not be measured with Eurocentric standards. One dilemma that certainly must have crossed Boas's mind was whether he could, even as a supposedly objective white European, fully appreciate the nuances of nonwhite cultures.

One of the ways Boas addressed this dilemma was to use students who shared the ethnicity of the cultures he wanted to study. He relied on Ella Cara Deloria to get a window into the Native American culture of the Dakotas. As Deloria under Boas's influence wrote about Native American culture, so Zora Neale Hurston wrote about southern black culture.

Hurston had a unique relationship with Boas. As her teacher at Barnard College, he undoubtedly mesmerized her with his vast knowledge. Boas's belief in what Arnold Rampersad calls "cultural relativism" rang true with her as well, particularly because she came to New York in 1925 proud of her upbringing in all-black Eatonville.[5] But at the same time, Boas heightened Hurston's sense of cultural irony. This sense of cultural irony does not seem as pronounced as her sense of racial irony until one reads Hurston's magnum opus of African American folk culture, *Mules and Men.*

First published in 1935, the book contains two major sections: "Folk Tales" and "Hoodoo" (hoodoo is synonymous with voodoo). In the preface to *Mules and Men,* Boas explains why Hurston's book of folklore surpasses Joel Chandler Harris's in its accuracy:

> Ever since the time of Uncle Remus, Negro folklore has exerted a strong attraction upon the imagination of the American public. Negro tales, songs and sayings without end, as well as descriptions of Negro magic and voodoo, have appeared; but in all of them the *intimate* setting in the social life of the Negro has never been given adequately. (xiii, emphasis added)

Boas assumes that Hurston's experiment in folklore has the benefit of an intimacy Harris could not claim. No matter how meticulous Harris might have been, he still could not have fully identified with the people of whom he wrote. Supposedly, Hurston could. That Hurston wrote a more "intimate" account of southern black life than her white predecessor is also reflected in the narrative itself. The readers practically witness the setting and the gathering process for the tales Hurston wrote. When she went south, she was returning home and therefore established a degree of credibility for her subjects and to her readers.

More to the point, Boas implies that Hurston did a better job than Harris did because she is black. Since *Mules* begins in Eatonville and continues through segregated African American communities in the South, Boas may have a point. The irony is that he as a white man must verify the authenticity of Hurston's account, similar to the white abolitionists who wrote prefaces in order to authenticate slave narratives during the nineteenth century.

Hurston was aware of this problem, which is probably why *Mules* sometimes departs from standard ethnographic writing. There are definite moments within the book when one is not sure whether Hurston is writing a novel or a factual account. This leads me to the statement to which I alluded in the title of this chapter—"You can read my words, but you can't read my mind." Within the context of this remark, Hurston addresses how southern rural blacks typically responded to whites objectifying black culture. The key was to stage for whites the daily activities of southern black life without the whites becoming aware that such staging was taking place.

The issue, then, is not Hurston's genre violations but rather the question, can anyone outside a marginalized culture accurately represent that culture? Even Boas, with his "objective" approach to ethnography, remains an outsider to the culture he studies. More profoundly, in one sense, so did Hurston as his student.

Hurston had an intellectual and existential investment in the African American folk culture that she represented in her writing. This fact separates her from Chesnutt and Du Bois. As a result, she possessed an appreciation for even the presumed "primitive" elements of that culture, like hoodoo. But curiously, Hurston's intimacy with black folk culture accentuates her awareness of the faint line between insider and outsider. Or as Johnson reveals,

> Yet the terms "black" and "white," "inside," and "outside," continue to matter. Hurston suspends the certainty of reference not by erasing these differences but by foregrounding the complex dynamism of their interaction.[6]

Black Culture and White Culture: Independent or Interdependent?

Hurston's perspective on African American culture, therefore, was more balanced than those held by Chesnutt and Du Bois. We should appreciate Chesnutt and Du Bois for introducing their readers to the value of cultural contributions made by African Americans. However, as I have shown in chapters 3 and 4, it was hardly their intention to place these contributions in the same class as Euro-American contributions. Particularly, African American folk traditions were valuable insofar as they enabled white America to see a significant, and often unrecognized, side of the larger American cultural milieu. Both Chesnutt and Du Bois, then, saw African American culture as subordinate to, as well as serving, Euro-American culture.

In contrast, Hurston did not devalue African American folk tradition as she introduced her readers to it. Nor did she devalue Euro-American culture. Hurston was the first to completely break away from mainstream artistic uses of black dialect. Gayl Jones cites Hurston's "The Gilded Six Bits" as among the first examples of an artist employing dialect not only through character dialogue but also to frame the narrative.

Gates coins "free indirect discourse" to explain the strategy Hurston uses in *Their Eyes Were Watching God* to mediate between the narrator's use of standardized American English and the characters' use of AAVE.[7] When Gates refers to the "voice" of the protagonist Janie, he means voice not only as "point of view" but also as the sociolinguistic "representation" of dialect within fiction (*Signifying* 181). In this way, dialect becomes, at least within Hurston's narrative, an alternative manifestation of public literacy, hence a type of "voicing." As such, the "voice of the narrative commentary" is acceptable, since it refers to the narrator's specific viewpoint, ascertainable from the text itself.

Curiously, Gates leaves the concrete confines of sociolinguistics and literary narrative to describe Hurston's unique voice:

> The narrative voice Hurston created, and her legacy to Afro-American fiction, is a lyrical and disembodied yet individual voice, from which emerges a singular longing utterance, a transcendent, ultimately racial self, extending far beyond the merely individual. Hurston realized a resonant and authentic narrative voice that echoes and aspires to the status of the impersonality, anonymity, and authority of the black vernacular tradition, a nameless, selfless tradition, at once collective and compelling, true somehow to the unwritten text of a common blackness. (*Signifying* 183)

Exactly how one would translate this passage for writers of color trying to find their voice is beyond me. I only mention this fact now because Gates's book is often referenced by writing teachers who are trying to learn how to better serve African American students, as well as to introduce other writers to African American vernacular strategies that could be used in writing.

The passage is laden with the same type of racial generalization that I critiqued in chapter 2 and that Gates himself critiques in the sixth chapter of *The Signifying Monkey*. That Gates may be suggesting, among other matters, the broad utility of black vernacular does not in any way render without theoretical limitation his employing phrases like "transcendent, ultimately racial self," or "the unwritten text of common blackness."

Granted, most of Hurston's works, from *Jonah's Gourd Vine* to *Their Eyes Were Watching God* and *Mules and Men,* celebrate the vitality and power of the southern black idiom. What makes the praise about Hurston especially striking is that it appears (in the texts mentioned) to be based on a self-contained analysis of black idiom. That is, AAVE is not valuable in comparison with or because it is superior to white uses of language—it is valuable on its own merits. And this constitutes one of the differences between Hurston's take on dialect and Chesnutt's. For Chesnutt, AAVE is primarily a class marker, even though it possesses artistic value. For Hurston, it is almost exclusively a cultural marker. On a literary level, class is incidental to that form of language that is richly interwoven into the fabric of southern black society.

Hurston's analysis of and appreciation for black idiom was fairly consistent. Her essay "The Characteristics of Negro Expression" underscores the facility with metaphor, imagery, and neologism Hurston observed in southern black communities. She illustrated how southern blacks enliven the language by transforming nouns into verbs. This becomes an even more striking observation given two statements H. L. Mencken makes in *The American Language:* (1) one of the characteristics that distinguishes American English from British English is the creative way in which Americans turn nouns into verbs, and (2) blacks have not contributed to the development of the American language.[8]

One incident from *Dust Tracks,* however, complicates such an assessment of Hurston's views on AAVE. During her young adult life, Hurston briefly joined an orchestra. The other members, white northerners, teased Hurston about her manner of speech, to which she retorted that both black and white southerners spoke the way she did. While it is indeed true that Hurston honors southern black folk idiom, there are, as far as I can tell, no passages where she details how this speech differs from that of southern whites of similar background. For Hurston, there may be some clear distinctions; however, I find it intriguing that these are not clearly discussed throughout her writings.

With regard to black idiom and culture, Hurston may be playing the same ironic game she plays with race. One moment she speaks of African American cultural and linguistic independence, the next of cultural and linguistic interdependence between southern black and white speech. Hurston's last published fictional work, *Seraph on the Suwanee,* substantiates the plausibility of this position. The story centers on two poor, white Floridians and their tumultuous courtship and marriage. This was the only novel Hurston wrote in which whites are the central characters.

As Hazel Carby notes, "the language," and in some cases, "whole phrases" of the dialogue the white characters utter in *Suwanee* do not contrast significantly with that black Floridians practice in *Their Eyes Were Watching God* (ix). Yet Carby sees the linguistic structure of the dialogue and the question of Hurston's ability to write about southern white characters as secondary to a much larger point. Karla Holloway concurs partly when she opines, "Hurston has not written a white text, nor has she written a black one in white face" (74). For Hurston, race, region, and class were a part of the larger cultural contributors to the formation of language and identity. Carby remarks,

> Hurston aimed to make *Seraph on the Suwanee* "a true picture of the South." She was delighted that Burroughs Mitchell was impressed with her use of Southern vernacular and idiom. In her previous novels and collection of folklore, *Mules and Men,* Hurston had established a reputation for her representation of black language and rhythms of speech. Though contemporary critics of Hurston's work have granted her a privileged position in the African American literary canon because of her sensitive delineation of black folk culture and black folk consciousness, particularly through language, Hurston's own views are more complex and controversial. In writing *Seraph on the Suwanee,* Hurston repudiated theories of the uniqueness of black linguistic structures. (viii)

In a letter to Burroughs Mitchell, an editor for Charles Scribner's Sons, Hurston said "that what is known as the Negro dialect in the South is no such thing" (Carby viii). Of course, we have known for decades that Hurston was mistaken in downplaying uniqueness of black dialect. Nevertheless, with this remark, Hurston interrogates the idea that black dialect developed in total isolation.

One should not conclude from this letter, therefore, that Hurston devalues completely the contribution that blacks made to the English language from within their segregated communities. As I noted above, Hurston's essay "Characteristics of Negro Expression" attests to specific instances of the African American linguistic nexus to standardized English. However, I think it would be even more accurate to say that with *Seraph*, Hurston strove to expose the unrecognized and unacknowledged moments of cultural amalgamation between whites and blacks.

Hurston did not deem this recognition of cultural amalgamation as mutually exclusive to her celebration of black folk culture. She could be black without accepting "blackness" as an objective reality. She could celebrate the unique worth of black culture while recognizing its, in some cases, elusive interconnectedness to white culture.

A seriously playful irony, then, marks Hurston's critique of race, language, and culture. For Hurston, all three were matters of stance, matters of performance. Thus she found no difficulty in violating the rules of genre, sexual taboos, and racial stereotypes. She was most comfortable with ambiguity. As a result, Hurston was not preoccupied with proving herself, as was Du Bois, making sure white society beheld her best side. Like Hughes, she believed that blacks should express "their natural dark-skinned selves."

Hurston's view of culture, like that of Du Bois, was inextricably tied to her view of race. But her appreciation for African American folk culture was not sacrificed in the process. In the end, Hurston neither inverted the white over black cultural hierarchy that has characterized this country nor would she. If race is a matter of "seeing and wearing," then culture too may be an unfixed matter of performance.

6

The Rhetoric of Black Voice:
Implications for Composition Pedagogy

THE METAPHOR "BLACK VOICE," WHETHER APPLIED to a journalist, a novelist, or a student writer, is based on two elusive ideas: voice and race. Hence, any concrete conclusions about the nature and function of black voice are questionable at best. Without this metaphor, however, one can appropriate a distorted view of both the material import and rhetorical efficacy of African American writing and culture. Ideally, alternative paradigms for black voice should acknowledge race as both abstract and rhetorically indispensable.

On the whole, rhetoric and composition scholars must become and remain more intentional in complicating the link between race and writing. Otherwise the field of composition studies can inadvertently reify the validity of racial boundaries codified from the 1870s through the 1920s and, theoretically by some, inverted during the 1960s. Granted, some rhetoric composition scholars, like Darsie Bowden, have noted that the late 1960s through the 1970s marked a pivotal point in the etymology of written voice, one in which the metaphor was broadened to include composition students. Indeed, in *The Mythology of Voice*, Bowden claims that prior to the 1960s, voice literally signified oral presentation (dating back to classical rhetoric) and figuratively signified authorial stance in traditional literary narrative. Bowden substantiates this claim by pinpointing a correlation between the sociopolitical challenges fos-

tered during the 1960s against all established institutions and an emerging student-centered pedagogy. This pedagogy would ideally replace
current traditional orthodoxy with an exploratory, neo-Romantic approach. As a result, teachers would honor the plethora of individual
student perspectives with the authorial designation "voice."

I concur with Bowden's major thesis that, for the most part, this neo-
Romantic legacy explains why voice as explicated currently within composition studies is a valuable yet problematical metaphor, one worthy
of the most rigorous, ongoing critique. And even though *The Mythology
of Voice* captures some of the larger cultural currents that led to the inception of voice as a metaphor within composition studies, the book
neglects to give adequate consideration to the marginalized groups that
came to voice during the 1960s. Bowden does include a chapter that
broaches the connections between women's studies and voice, a necessary
understanding to be sure; however, she merely grants passing acknowl-
edgement to the nuances of voice and race during the 1960s. Hence, for
my purposes, one of Bowden's major themes, namely how the voice
metaphor evolved beyond the purview of literature to encompass composition, must be complicated with a critical reflection on African American texts.

Black Arts Theory and Student Rights Pedagogy

The Black Arts movement, which lasted from the 1960s through the
1970s, was the second major African American literary movement. Considerably more political and, as I shall argue shortly, more narrowly
conceived than was the Harlem Renaissance, the social importance of
the Black Arts movement nevertheless can be hardly overstated. This
artistic movement shaped and was shaped by a critical sociopolitical
consciousness. These were the days of boycotts, sit-ins, freedom rides,
student demonstrations, and martyred civil rights leaders, and the days
for passionate spokespersons: Martin Luther King Jr., Malcolm X, Ruby
Doris Smith Robinson, Angela Davis, and Huey Newton, among many
others. Thus the leaders of the Black Arts movement gave voice to the
struggles, hopes, and joys of the black masses, to legitimize through literature their language, music, rituals, and traditions.

In this way, these writers sought to honor black folk culture as Hurston had done, their political agenda and focus on urban blacks notwith-

standing. Indeed, protest that results in revision of mainstream culture constitutes one of the major traditions in African American letters, the other being imitation of Euro-American discursive practices that leads to cultural assimilation. Even in terms of art exclusively, however, Black Arts writers had the right to protest the exclusion of literature written by people of color from the canon.

Other than scattered references to folk literature and a few black poets, for example, until 1971 articles in mainstream scholarly magazines generally failed to critically review works written by African Americans; the widespread fame of Richard Wright would constitute one of the few exceptions. Similarly, the National Council of Teachers of English published a survey indicating that through the 1950s, a person could presumably do an extensive study of the body of American literature without reading one African American writer.[1]

Obviously, then, Black Arts writers would more likely embrace as their role models revolutionaries demanding their rights on street corners rather than poets contemplating in the woods. Embracing the image of the revolutionary writer is not a drawback in itself. That is to say, most of the time it is legitimate, even desirable, for literature to serve a social function.[2] Instead, the problem during the Black Arts movement became the ways in which racial propaganda delimited the identity of the African American writer.[3] Related to this issue is a question: who has the right to be the arbiter of authentic black identity and writing?

Barbara Christian introduces the substance of this question into postmodern discussions of literary theory. Her "Race for Theory," which first appeared in *Culture Critique* in 1987, proposes to "break the silence" for those critics, such as herself, who "have been intimidated, devalued by . . . the race for theory" (348). For Christian, the deifying of postmodern literary theory devalues primary texts in that the contemporary scholar feels more obligated to analyze what other critics have said about texts than what the authors themselves say. Moreover, in the postmodern move to open up primary texts to multiple readings, a type of elitism has evolved in which certain texts, many written by African Americans, never received close readings in the *traditional* sense.

This trend leads Christian to a critique of postmodern theory, not for the myriad questions provoked by its introduction into the academy but for the "prescriptiveness" that in many cases has resulted from its uninhibited reign. To rephrase, the interpretive freedom represented by semantic indeterminacy and endless signifiers paradoxically enslaves one to a kind of reading, which by definition must proscribe any reading that assumes meaning can be found. Christian contends that a group of black authors fell into this trap as well:

> An example of this prescriptiveness is the approach the Black Arts Movement took towards language. For it, blackness resided in the use of black talk, which they defined as hip urban language. So that when Nikki Giovanni reviewed Paule Marshall's *Chosen Place, Timeless People,* she criticized the novel on the grounds it wasn't black, for the language was too elegant, too white. Blacks, she said, did not speak that way. Having come from the West Indies where we do, some of the time, speak that way, I was amazed at the narrowness of her vision. The emphasis on *one* way to be black resulted in the works of Southern writers being seen as non-black since the black talk of Georgia does not sound like the black talk of Philadelphia. Because the ideologues, like Baraka, came from the urban centers, they tended to privilege their way of speaking, thinking, writing, and to condemn other kinds of writing as not black enough. . . . Older writers like Ralph Ellison and James Baldwin were condemned because they saw that the intersection of Western and African influences resulted in a new Afro-American culture. (354–55)

Overlooking the "intersection" between the Western and African strains of African American culture was a gross misreading. Assuming, as some of the leaders of this movement evidently did, that a few African Americans could arbitrate what constituted authentic black literature and identity was far more presumptuous.

By including Baraka, Ellison, and Baldwin, Christian further exposes this presumption. Amiri Baraka (known as LeRoi Jones until 1967) was considered one of the founders of and spokespersons for the Black Arts movement. His play *Dutchman,* written in 1964, set the tone for the movement, as it denied the practicality of integration.[4] And although Baraka produced books of poetry, plays, and a few collections of essays, eventually replacing his Black Arts Nationalism with Marxism, the significance of his work during this period pales in comparison to that of Ellison and Baldwin. Ellison and Baldwin more accurately describe the "intersection between Western and African influences" of which Christian speaks, an intersection shaped by what Eric Sundquist calls the historical "dialectic" between black and white cultures.

Ralph Ellison, the author of one of the greatest modern novels, *Invisible Man,* held to a dialectical take on black culture specifically and American culture generally. During the 1960s, he differed with those who rejected the melting pot as a metaphor for America. He saw this rejection as "an effort to dismiss the mystery of American identity (our unity—within diversity)" ("Little" 25). For Ellison, the melting pot did not represent the loss of ethnic identity, therefore, but the tense, yet essential, interplay among minority cultures (and Ellison would include white culture within this definition) in the formation of a new, larger American culture. Further, this mutual cultural interchange (between whites and blacks, for instance) would exist regardless of whether either group recognized it.[5]

Likewise, James Baldwin's novels and essays advocate racial equality. However, he further complicates the distinctions among race, gender, and sexual orientation.[6] Baldwin's sexual orientation contributed more to the Black Arts ideologues' rejection of his work than did his belief in the "intersection" between Western and African cultures. Baldwin was openly gay during a time when homosexuals were more oppressed than they are presently. In fact, he preferred the designation "homosexual" over "gay," as he thought the latter term simply euphemized and, as a result, detracted from the stark reality of his sexuality. It is not surprising that the homophobia that characterized some black militant thinking during the 1960s was leveled against Baldwin in a number of bigoted ways.

What Phillip Brian Harper has argued, therefore, regarding Black Arts poetry specifically can be said, to some degree, of the Black Arts movement generally. Its aesthetic reflects a troubling paradox: promoting Black nationalistic unity at the price of intraracial division, antigay sentiments being one of the clearest lines. And I contend that the lines that would myopically demarcate black identity and aesthetics could theoretically extend to racialized writing irrespective of genre.

In part because some sexist and homophobic Black Arts ideologues spoke as the arbiters of black identity, not to mention the literature that should be written about that identity, the New Black Aesthetic emerged.

Indeed, unlike the Black Arts movement yet like the Harlem Renaissance, some of the most prominent members of the New Black Aesthetic movement were gay, like George Wolfe. According to Henry Louis Gates Jr., this movement destabilized the borders of black identity posited during the Black Arts movement. In effect, the New Black Aesthetic mirrors "[t]he range of representations of the meaning of blackness among the post–*Song of Solomon* (1978) era of black writing" (*Loose* 143). Trey Ellis articulates the movement's thinking when he says, "The New Black Aesthetic says you have to *be* natural, you don't necessarily have to *wear* one." Unlike their counterparts in the Black Arts movement, Ellis and other proponents of this new aesthetic are indifferent to what white people think (*Loose* 145). That is, their art is defined neither in terms of protest against nor in reverent imitation of mainstream discourse.

Gates argues that "points of a post–Black Aesthetic triangle" include Ellis's satire and manifesto "The New Black Aesthetic," Toni Morrison's cutting-edge attempt to transcend the "ultimate horror of black past— slavery" in her novel *Beloved*, and C. Eric Lincoln's effort to maintain "black vernacular culture . . . for a younger generation." I am particularly interested in the satirical scrutiny of the Black Arts movement essentialism. Like Ellis, George C. Wolfe wrote *The Colored Museum* in the 1980s to address the complexities of black identity. The following vignette from *The Colored Museum* illuminates the worth of this enterprise:

> But now let me tell you 'bout this function I went to the other night, way uptown. And baby when I say way uptown, I mean way-way-way-way-way-way-way-way uptown. Somewhere's between 125th Street and infinity. Inside was the largest gathering of black/Negro/colored Americans you'd ever want to see. Over in one corner you got Nat Turner sippin' champagne out of Eartha Kitt's slipper. And over in another corner, Bert Williams and Malcolm X was discussing existentialism as it relates to the shuffle-ball-change. Girl, Aunt Jemima and Angela Davis was in the kitchen sharing a plate of greens and just goin' off about South Africa. (50)

Using hyperbole, Wolfe chides efforts, such as those enacted in the Black Arts movement, to conclusively define black culture. He juxtaposes opposite character types, time periods, and regions to highlight this absurdity.

Bert Williams, one of the first black minstrels, would not be found in the company of Malcolm X, even if the two men were contemporaries. The same holds true for Aunt Jemima and Angela Davis. More striking still, Malcolm X and Angela Davis, active participants and, some would contend, icons of the Black Arts movement are paired with stereotypical images, Bert Williams and Aunt Jemima. Of course, existentialism bears no obvious ideological link to the type of party dancing mentioned.

Wolfe's conflating of "black/Negro/colored," however, perhaps comprises the most telling part of the passage. The first racial representation emerges last historically, and in juxtaposing all of these representations at the beginning of the passage, Wolfe constructs the setting for the shifting among time, region, and character he discusses throughout the piece.

Gates considers Ellis and Wolfe as heirs to Ishmael Reed's satirical tradition. Reed's *Mumbo Jumbo* was published in 1972 near the end of the Black Arts movement. The book mocks the Western literary tradition, the Harlem Renaissance, and the Black Arts movement, suggesting that academic, literary, and folk discourses are racialized. Thereby, Reed speaks to the historical contexts of these literary traditions and exposes the rhetorics produced by them. He exposes a cultural communication gap between blacks and whites, based partly on the whites' inability to comprehend the essence of black language and literature and partly on the blacks' assumption that such an essence exists to begin with.[7] Reed evinces the arbitrariness of academic discourse and literary traditions by obfuscating genre restrictions. The book is a work of fiction, yet it contains footnotes and a partial bibliography. In the same manner, it defies arrangement. The book includes sections written in cursive and depicting charts. Chapter 1 begins before the title page and another page listing Reed's previous works.

Reed's book affords the same opportunity for playful constructions of identity that I examined in Hurston's writing. Hurston also played with genre restrictions or the rhetoric of genre—writers should not be controlled by genre but rather should control genre to accomplish their aims. This is why Reed blurs the distinctions between factual and fictional writing.

Most important, Reed criticizes the act of writing during the Harlem Renaissance and the Black Arts movement by writing.[8] The act of writing racialized discourse minimizes the importance of genre and technique. The power is in the staging itself.

The leaders of the New Black Aesthetic movement made an essential move in questioning narrow definitions of sociopolitical and artistic voice among African Americans. However, these writers could have sufficiently strengthened their argument, which is really about black identity, by rigorously questioning what constitutes blackness itself. Like Du Bois, Wolfe, for example, destabilizes race designations but does not transcend them. Still another necessary step for the New Black literati could have been to offer an alternative paradigm of authorship. It is insufficient to parody the folly of static designations of race and voice without discussing how these two concepts might be reconstructed while maintaining useful community.

Two years after *Mumbo Jumbo* was published in literary circles, "The Students' Right to Their Own Language" was published by the Conference on College Composition and Communication. In fact, in a recent *CCC* article, Geneva Smitherman suggests that "The Students' Right" emerged from the same sociopolitical context that gave rise to the Black Arts movement. The introduction to the 1974 document emphasizes, among other matters, rhetoric and composition scholars' commitment to teaching a linguistically diverse student population:

> Differences in language have always existed, and the schools have always wrestled with them, but the social upheavals of the 1960s, and the insistence of submerged minorities on a greater share in American society have suggested the need for a shift in emphasis in providing answers. Should the schools try to uphold language variety, or to modify it, or to eradicate it? (*Students'* 10)

By recognizing this "shift in emphasis," the writers of this document demonstrated their sensitivity to diverse social and academic concerns. Such sensitivity, of course, resonates with the rhetorical tradition of finding the social value in a variety of discourses. The question raised at the end of the above paragraph seems to evoke the options that writing teachers wishing to address linguistic diversity must address.

As one might expect, the document's design also reflects this sensitivity. A thorough document, "Students' Right to Their Own Language" poses and offers preliminary answers to fifteen questions that were and are socially, politically, and pedagogically relevant. These questions address issues such as defining dialect, determining the impact of dialect on the acquisition of literacy, and how adopting a liberal approach to linguistic diversity might affect the use of composition handbooks and standardized tests. In its articulate explication and defense of linguistic diversity, therefore, the document remains one of the profoundest repudiations of current traditional rhetoric. Like Sharon Crowley's *Methodical Memory*, "The Students' Right to Their Own Language" contests the notion that edited American English is essentially democratic and culturally inclusive. Crowley argues that current traditionalism evolved in part from eighteenth-century epistemology and British new rhetoric, so that by the twentieth century, current traditional textbooks had supplanted the teacher's authority and the student writer's discursive individuality.

Of course, the historical flash points for "The Students' Rights to Their Own Language" and for Crowley's book differ. Nevertheless, by affirming the communicative efficacy of the student dialects of many ethnic groups, the document too deconstructs the assumption that there is an inherently transcending worth in standardized American correctness. Hence, the document covers a wide terrain, from fundamental definitions to more advanced implications. Indeed, postmodernists (who supposedly stress both sensitivity to and the endless pursuit of plurality) would applaud some of the observations made in the document. For example, like Michel Foucault, the writers of "Students' Right to Their Own Language" consider knowledge, in this case the privileging of standardized American English, the reflection of the hierarchy of power.[9]

The major premises of the document, sensitive awareness to linguistic diversity and recognition of the potential pedagogical value of student dialects, remain fundamental to any successful composition program. More important, the document calls current rhetoric-composition professors, as Patrick Bruch and Richard Marback have argued, to acknowledge the history of "rights rhetoric" in this country and to advocate a philosophy of literacy that wages ongoing battles for the individual liberties and civil rights of the disenfranchised.

In a few ways, however, the document could be construed to inadvertently create the same shaky ideological foundation for composition pedagogy as the Black Arts movement did for literary studies. For one thing, focusing on the existential investment students have in their respective dialects could ironically restrict pedagogical discussion. Accordingly, teachers are primarily responsible for cultivating the students' "self-esteem and self-image" by giving ample respect to their dialects. As a result, this becomes one of the places where "Students' Right to Their Own Language" appears confusing. Precisely, how are these various dialects to be honored existentially? I ask this question in terms of purpose and pragmatics. If one of the original intentions of the document were to affirm the linguistic diversity of our student population, wouldn't one also need to affirm linguistic diversity within a given racial or ethnic group? Moreover, given the historical moment when the "Students' Right to Their Own Language" emerged, shouldn't we be open to interrogating the document for ideological remnants of the groupthink that to some degree characterized the Black Arts movement?

As composition-rhetoric teachers, our primary mandate is to affirm the communicative efficacy of AAVE while emphasizing the rhetorical value of standardized American English. To teach standardized American English is not necessarily to denigrate AAVE. What could have been stressed more in this document is that edited American English should be acknowledged and taught as *one* rhetorical strategy.

In short, while "The Students' Right to Their Own Language" made avant-garde contributions to race, language, culture, politics, and pedagogy, the document fell short of sufficiently complicating the links among race, language, and identity for peoples of color. The neo-Expressionist impulse that was already gaining ground in composition studies during the 1960s and 1970s was and can continue to be further complicated by race.[10] Revisiting seminal documents like "The Students' Rights" can either help or hinder composition scholars in avoiding full appropriation of a Romantic-racialized take on voice.[11]

"Walkin' the Walk or Talkin' Whose Talk?": Gender, Vernacular, and Afrocentric Composition

Since the publication of "Students' Rights," a number of stellar publications have explored African American dialect and writing pedagogy. *Tapping Potential,* which first appeared in 1985, remains worth considering. In fact, the essays in this collection written by Clara Franklin

Alexander, Jacqueline Jones Royster, and Robert J. Fowler are especially pertinent for understanding dialect pedagogy.

One could hardly overstate the past and present pedagogical benefits of black dialect studies. Scholars as diverse as Geneva Smitherman, William Labov, Shirley Brice Heath, Keith Gilyard, Arnetha Ball, John Rickford, and most recently, Elaine Richardson, not to mention a host of others, have radically improved writing assessment and instruction. Nevertheless, the question remains, how do composition teachers get their students to realize simultaneously the complexity and utility of constructing a racialized ethos? To broach this question, I turn to three essays, which are meant only to be representative, illustrative rather than comprehensive, of a few of the elusive yet material boundaries—gender, language, and geography—that simultaneously inform and are informed by racialized writing.

Juanita Rodgers Comfort's "Becoming a Writerly Self: Engaging Black Feminist Essays" makes a compelling argument for what I call a "topoi of difference" in composition pedagogy. According to Comfort, one paradoxical way to enable our students to enter into the shared arena of public academic discourse is to have them engage essays of personal reflection on race and gender. The core of Comfort's essay illustrates how she uses June Jordan's "Requiem for the Champ" to communicate the above notion to her graduate students.

Since "Requiem" entails a sketch of Mike Tyson that appears sympathetic to him, Comfort's graduate students, particularly one white woman, found it difficult to connect with Jordan, even though they shared the same gender. Comfort further discusses how she led this student through a number of rhetorical mazes to get to Jordan's point. Clearly, Jordan does not defend Tyson's transgressions but rather identifies, empathetically to be sure, with his socioeconomic plight shaped by his race. Hence Jordan's work enacts for Comfort's student a valuable lesson about ethos: it is best constructed as the writer demonstrates that connection to and conflict with one's subject can coexist.

Through a close reading of "Requiem," then, Comfort's student comes to appreciate the pathos achievable through the topoi of difference. This topoi of difference constitutes one of the reasons why Comfort's essay is so valuable. The essay complicates the easy dichotomies often drawn between public and private discourse as well as between race and gender.

Obviously, Comfort is aware of the materiality of the differences entailed in categories of race, gender, and class; however she argues that if negotiated skillfully, these differences will not only bridge the path between writer and audience but will also help to shape the course of that path. In light of the fact that for decades, the personal experiences of white males have informed the definition of public discourse, her claim is sound.

In short, Comfort's topoi of difference can function as a heuristic for the construction of diverse types of ethos. That is, from a particular construction of ethos, one shaped by race, gender, and class, Comfort provides general methodology for framing writers' varying personal markers, and thereby demonstrates those rhetors' limited but real potential to manipulate these markers. But the question becomes, does Comfort introduce adequately the extent of diversity necessary to the construction of ethos? Granted she explicates the impact of interracial and intergender differences on ethos and pathos. I just wish she had broached a similar analysis of intraracial and intragender differences.

Kermit E. Campbell's essay "'Real Niggaz's Don't Die': African American Students Speaking Themselves into Their Writing" underscores the importance of writing teachers allowing African American students to incorporate Black English vernacular strategies into their essays. Campbell centers on the vernacular strategy "signifying." A richly layered term, *signifying* is what Henry Louis Gates Jr. styles "the master trope" of African American culture. Campbell defines the layers of signifying he will examine when he, referring to Geneva Smitherman, says that "the term usually refers to 'the verbal art of insult in which a speaker puts down, talks about, needles—that is, signifies on—the listener'" (Smitherman 118, qtd. in Campbell 67).

Through his protocol studies of several African American male college students in the Midwest, Campbell details how these students might signify in academic prose. In personal narratives, for example, they could demonstrate their mastery of figurative language by employing lively metaphors they coined on the street (Campbell 71–73). Likewise, even these students' (and other African Americans') use of the word *nigga* instead of *nigger* evinces their facility to adapt a pejorative term and make it a fraternal term.

Moreover, Campbell offers a convincing rationale for signifying as a pedagogical strategy. Allowing "nonmainstream" students to utilize ver-

bal strategies, such as signifying, will legitimize and affirm "their social
and cultural identities" (69). Campbell goes on to discuss two assignments
that move the students toward these goals. The students may write eth-
nographies. The students should also read famous African American auto-
biographies, which Campbell acknowledges as a site for validating AAVE.

Overall, Campbell's enterprise is theoretically and pedagogically sound.
As rhetoric-composition scholars, we have yet to fully honor the vernacular of our students. More to the point, we have deprived our students
of the opportunity to expand their rhetorical arsenal with the striking
flexibility that vernacular affords.

But Campbell's take on African American autobiography actually inhib-
its his project. Granted, African American autobiography showcases the
literary and linguistic efficacy of dialect. This genre, however, also stresses
the ability of blacks to master and manipulate any discursive strategy,
including so-called standard American English. How "affirmed" would
black students be when they discover that one of their heroes, Malcolm
X, not only easily code-shifted from standardized to vernacular speech but
also was among the first to employ effectively the sound bites and the
rapid-fire verbal exchange that characterize current political discourse?

Like Campbell's essay, Henry L. Evans's "An Afrocentric Multicultural Writing Project" addresses some of the ethnocentric assumptions
that govern our approach to teaching African American student writers.
Moreover, Evans shares Barbara Christian's skepticism about the relationship of postmodernism to African American intellectual traditions:

> While Afrocentrics respond to poststructuralist critiques, they
> must recognize that the core white, Western, and European
> self identity (male and female), however complex it is or what-
> ever the amount of influx and shifting occurs, remains solid,
> intact, the same long-established power and privilege in re-
> lation to peoples of color. No European American refuses (or
> decenters from) the birth-certificate right that identifies him
> or her as white and that secures the lifelong legal, social, and
> psychological privileges accompanying white identity. (275)

Evans's concerns, however, are culturally broader than Christian's or
Campbell's. Evans wishes to do more than expand black literary sensi-
bilities beyond the Black Arts movement (Christian) or include vernacu-

lar traditions in teaching writing (Campbell). Evans contends that an Afrocentric worldview should significantly inform writing theory and pedagogy. By attempting to "decenter" all ideologies, postmodernists trivialize the extent to which Afrocentrism can account for divergent thinking styles, enhance students' self-esteem, and improve "student-teacher relationship." Hence an Afrocentric worldview "situates" and empowers African American students in ways that Euro-American students have always been.

Evans's analysis of African and European thinking styles is particularly helpful. Borrowing from the research on cognition performed by African American psychologist James Anderson, Evans contrasts "holistic" and "analytic" thinking styles. The first tends to be more communal, frequently adopting the second-person pronoun, indicative of the African influence on the way some African Americans think. Analytic thinkers, in keeping with their European heritage, easily appropriate third person in their writing. As Evans rightly notes, knowledge of these thinking styles would greatly assist a writing teacher in teaching revision, among other things (279–80).

Yet Evans's project actually may not be as inclusive as it appears to be at first glance. Certainly composition teachers should follow Evans's lead and seek the insights an Afrocentric worldview ensures. But can we do so while explicitly and implicitly avoiding facile notions of what constitutes African American identity? Do students cease to be authentically black if they fail to identify with mother Africa in the way Professor Evans or others deems that they should? Can these students who have different takes on Africa benefit from the rhetorical insights generated from an Afrocentric worldview?

Taken together, Comfort's, Campbell's, and Evans's respective arguments only begin, as this book has, to broach the complexities of constructing black ethos in writing, complexities that remain informed by, at the very least, the dialectic between African and European cultures, rather than only the distinctiveness of each culture. We should also consider the ways African American culture has contributed and continues to contribute to the evolution of so-called standard American English. Granted, the distinctions between standardized American English and AAVE (especially syntactic and phonologic distinctions) are irrefutable linguistically. Yet forging total distinctions between standard English and

AAVE can be problematic rhetorically. As writing teachers, we should avoid leaving our African American students with the impression that standardized American English is any less their intellectual property because it has been used to disenfranchise them.

Perhaps the rhetorical theories Berlin posits in *Rhetoric and Reality*— "objective," "subjective," and "transactional"—provide one heuristic for beginning to interrogate the gist of my concerns about racialized voice. From an objective point of view, voice can mainly be manifested by language structures (phonology, morphology, syntax, semantics, and pragmatics). From a subjective standpoint, voice can be a fervent yet elusive attempt to capture the collective consciousness of a people, or it can refer to an individual's or community's right to speak. And a transactional view makes voice a negotiated construct among addressers, as well as between addresser and addressee. In essence, I have argued that we must continue to explore the richness of the objective and transactional aspects of black voice without sacrificing subjective notions of personally and communally constructed racialized voice on the altar of group ontology.

Therefore, composition scholars should continue to creatively incorporate the African American oral tradition into their classrooms. Students should listen to and, in most cases, see and listen to (via audio, video, and hypertext) the great sermons, speeches, and songs of African America. For one reason, our students' perceptions of American culture and so-called standard language are distorted without this exposure. More important, the students will realize that they can barely fathom the richness of a tradition that was meant to be heard and not read, spoken and not written. W. Ross Winterowd's claim that one cannot capture the nuances of voice in any concrete form in writing applies markedly more to layered African American orality.

Race as a way of reading introduces historical, ideological, and pedagogical vistas to addressing the dilemma that I posed in chapter 2. As rhetoric and composition scholars, we must recognize the ubiquity of intellectual and material racism. But we must also remain aware of the culturally embedded impulse to link race, language, and identity. And this meta-awareness should inform our thinking and teaching, particularly about race and constructing ethos. Race is not merely rhetorical, but we must continue to empower our students to explore race rhetorically.

Notes
Works Cited and Consulted
Index

Notes

Introduction

1. See Erich Segal's introduction to *The Dialogues of Plato*, Bantam ed.

2. The simultaneous elevation of inspiration and denigration of invention are key concepts in W. Ross Winterowd's work.

3. For a more detailed discussion of the One Mind, consult the section entitled "Consciousness" in ch. 1 of Matthiessen 5–14.

1. The Color of Literacy: Race, Self, and the Public Ethos

1. Sundquist's first chapter in *To Wake the Nations* remains among the best scholarship on Douglass. Particularly engaging is Sundquist's argument regarding how Douglass seeks to revise societal perceptions of his own racial identity as well as the slave insurrections, so that the Americanness of both enterprises becomes evident.

2. See William L. Andrews's introduction to *Critical Essays on Frederick Douglass* and John Blassingame's introduction to *The Frederick Douglass Papers*, vol. 1.

3. *Heteroglossia*, a pivotal theoretical term in Bakhtin's work, is predictably among the most difficult of his concepts to grasp. The reader is encouraged, therefore, to consult Bakhtin's *Dialogic Imagination* in its entirety.

2. From Reading Race to Race as a Way of Reading

1. I adapt the idea "race as a hermeneutic" from Uzo Esonwanne. There are, however, a few principal differences between his use of the phrase and mine. For example, he is concerned neither with replacing the metaphor of race as a text with race as a hermeneutic nor with the implications of race as a hermeneutic for constructing authorship generally and for composition theory specifically. Moreover, although Esonwanne begins suggesting a basis for cultural critique, his analysis is more philosophical, global, and less taken with rethinking American social history than is mine. Most important, he does not expose the fallacies associated with other figurative readings of race. See Esonwanne.

2. See the first chapter of Stanton and ch. 3 of Gossett.

3. The cursory discussion that unfolds here is largely taken from Thomas F. Gossett's and William Stanton's respective treatises. In ch. 4 of his book, Gossett provides a more focused treatment of the rise of the polygenetic view than

Stanton does. Nevertheless, Stanton's remarks, which are scattered throughout his book, are also somewhat helpful.

4. Note the arguments Ann Douglas and Michael North make respectively in *Terrible Honesty*, ch. 2, and *The Dialect of Modernism*, ch. 1.

5. Du Bois, a contemporary of James Weldon Johnson's, virtually eliminated dialect from his fiction, as he believed that in using it, he would perpetuate the stereotype of the "ignorant Negro."

6. See chs. 1 and 5 of Jones's *Liberating Voices*.

7. Eric Sundquist has provided a most insightful discussion on this case. See *To Wake the Nations*, ch. 3.

8. Consult Fauset, "The Negro, the Blue Man, and the New Race" (sec. 3 of Rusch); and Larsen's *Quicksand* and *Passing*.

9. See also *The Philosophy of Alain Locke* (L. Harris 31, 284).

10. Consult Huggins.

11. For an appreciation of the context of this observation, see Zack, ch. 10.

12. Toomer spent most of his life vacillating between various racial and ethnic designations, even though as early as 1914 he began pondering the concept "American race." Indeed, he took offense at being classified as a "Negro artist." Refer to Nellie Y. McKay's article on Toomer.

13. The editor of *"Race," Writing, and Difference*, Gates writes two essays that, like the entire collection, are worth greater consideration by composition scholars than is *The Signifying Monkey*. However, the latter has received more critical attention.

3. Chesnutt's Reconstruction of Race and Dialect

1. Compare Richard H. Brodhead's introduction to *The Conjure Woman and Other Conjure Tales* with ch. 4 of Donald B. Gibson's *The Politics of Literary Expression*.

2. Andrews's introduction to the *Collected Stories of Charles Chesnutt* (Mentor ed., 1992) suggests that Chesnutt's choice to reveal his race after the publication of *The Conjure Woman* collection was largely prompted by "Black readers and pundits" who "demanded that Chesnutt be recognized as an African American whose achievements spoke well of the artistic capabilities of people of color" (xiii).

3. Naomi Zack numbers Chesnutt among those "Black writers who were tolerant toward passing." She believes his tolerance stems from the "social chasm" he observed between light-skinned and dark-skinned blacks. Given Chesnutt's own social station and particularly his views on racial and cultural amalgamation, "empathetic" is a more appropriate description than is "tolerant."

4. J. Noel Heermance writes a helpful synopsis of the critical reception of Chesnutt's short stories, as well as how this reception moved Chesnutt into the role of racial spokesperson. What Heermance neglects to mention is that Chesnutt did not consider himself black. See Heermance, ch. 5.

5. Although he admired Harris's tales, Chesnutt sought to firmly establish the originality of his own. See Gibson 152, and his footnote to Chesnutt's "Post-Bellum Pre-Harlem."

6. J. L. Dillard errs in calling Harris one of those "children of the slave

owning class." He correctly notes that like those children, Harris "had plenty of opportunity to acquire Black English." See Dillard, ch. 5.

7. I based this conclusion partly on Houston Baker's remark that the animal tale is the best-known genre of African American folklore. See Baker, *Long*, ch. 2.

8. See Braithwaite. Aside from the reservations he has about the lack of literacy demonstrated by Uncle Remus, Braithwaite still lauds Harris's tales. For Braithwaite, Harris's characterization of Remus was "approaching a true portraiture," and Harris himself should be "regarded as a sort of providentially provided amanuensis for preserving the folk tales and legends of a race." What I consider Sterling Brown's greatest acknowledgment to Harris has gone largely unnoticed by contemporary scholars. Brown et al. included an excerpt from *Uncle Remus: His Songs and Sayings* in *The Negro Caravan*, an anthology of African American literature.

9. Refer to Shelley Fishkin's groundbreaking work, *Was Huck Black?*

10. Gayl Jones's *Liberating Voices* contains some scattered but helpful observations about Chesnutt's employment of dialect, particularly in the introduction and chs. 5 and 9. Eric J. Sundquist offers a more thorough discussion in ch. 4 of *To Wake the Nations*, although this chapter does not focus on dialect either.

11. William L. Andrews resonates this observation, adding that "*The Conjure Woman* evokes a world of mean-spirited, penny-pinching masters whose preoccupation with profit limits them to a narrow utilitarian attitude toward their slaves and life itself." For Donald B. Gibson, in contrast, Chesnutt partly "supports the values inherent in the traditions" of the Old South (128).

12. Dunbar wanted to be recognized for his lyrical poetry. However, his fame came from his dialect poetry. Chesnutt wrote dialect fiction simply to enter the literary marketplace. Once this was done, he went on to explore other genres.

13. *Mandy Oxendine* was Chesnutt's first novel, but publishers rejected it. The novel interrogates ideas of race and gender in ways that might give pause to critics of Chesnutt.

14. Donald Gibson employs *dialectical* to describe Chesnutt's divided regard for "the landed gentry," with whom he most identifies, and "the Black, landless peasant," for whom he "sympathizes." When I use *dialectic*, however, I am primarily interested in the way the two types of narratives within *The Conjure Woman* interact with each other.

15. Refer to Brodhead 10.

16. Consult Chesnutt's reception speech for the Spingarn Medal, given to him by the NAACP in 1928 (rpt. in Gibson 126).

4. Of Color and Culture: Du Bois's Evolving Perspectives on Race

1. I use the expression "autobiography proper" because Du Bois's earlier works, such as *The Souls of Black Folk*, contain autobiographical incidents. To explore the significance of this technique further, see Byerman, ch. 9.

2. As I observed earlier in this chapter, I am indebted to Kwame Anthony Appiah for his superb analysis of Du Bois's evolving understanding of race. See "Uncompleted" and "Conservation."

3. Kwame Anthony Appiah details the historical significance of the paper Du Bois presented during the first meeting of the American Negro Academy. See "Uncompleted" 23.

4. Refer to the analysis of Du Bois's *Dark Princess* and the footnote on *The Negro* in Rampersad, ch. 10.

5. According to Wilson J. Moses, Crummell was especially antagonistic toward biracial people. His relationship with Du Bois constituted one of the few exceptions to this rule. See Moses's introduction to Crummell.

6. Refer to ch. 1 of Lewis, *When*.

7. For a revealing study about the origin of many of Du Bois's operative terms, consult Zamir.

5. "Reading My Words but Not My Mind": Hurston's Ironic Voice

1. For a more developed discussion, consult Robert E. Hemenway's introduction to *Zora Neale Hurston: A Literary Biography*.

2 See Sundquist, *To*, ch. 1.

3. Some contemporary black conservatives hold positions similar to that of Hurston. Consider, for example, Thomas Sowell's views on affirmative action in *Civil Rights: Rhetoric or Reality?*

4. According to her biographer, Robert E. Hemenway, Hurston became so fed up with the art-as-propaganda contingent of the Harlem literary movement that she once declared, "I was and am thoroughly sick" of the "race problem." See Hemenway, *Zora*, ch. 2.

5. See Arnold Rampersad's foreword to the Harper Perennial edition of *Mules and Men* (1990).

6. In "Thresholds of Difference," Barbara Johnson explores Hurston's mediating role between insider and outsider. Worthy of particular note is the shift Johnson views Hurston making between using the "scientific narrative voice" of a folklore collector to including herself in the "we" voice of the blacks from whom she was collecting folklore. See specifically p. 139.

7. According to Gates, both Hurston's allegiance to and revision of black vernacular cannot be understood without understanding Free Indirect Discourse. See *Signifying*, ch. 5.

8. See Douglas, *Terrible*.

6. The Rhetoric of Black Voice: Implications for Composition Pedagogy

1. Paul Lauter's *Canons and Context* is a brilliant exposé of the politics of canonization. For a fuller discussion of the 1971 article on black authorship in the NCTE survey, consult ch. 2 of Lauter.

2. E.g., Kenneth Burke in *Counter-Statement*.

3. Two essay collections, *Black Fire* (ed. Leroi Jones and Larry Neal) and *The Black Aesthetic* (ed. Addison Gayle Jr.), reveal how pervasively black politics informed the artistic enterprise during the Black Arts movement.

4. Cf. Baraka.

5. For the most comprehensive treatment of what I call Ellison's take on "cultural amalgamation," consult his essay collection *Going to the Territory* (New York: Vintage, 1986).

6. The best textual illustration of Baldwin's life-long efforts to repudiate racism, sexism, and homophobia is his 1962 novel *Another Country.*

7. In *The Signifying Monkey,* Gates explains Reed's major strategies for critiquing the Western tradition, the Harlem Renaissance, and the Black Arts movement. The title *Mumbo Jumbo* refers both to whites' disdain for black culture and a Swahili term ("jambo and its plural, mambo") which means, "What's happening?" And in countering the Euro-American notion of "blackness as negative essence, as a natural transcendent, signified," Reed implicitly offers "a critique of blackness as a presence, which is merely another transcendent signified," a belief that was, to some degree, embraced during the Black Arts movement. The reader is encouraged to refer to Gates's cogent analysis of *Mumbo Jumbo* in *The Signifying Monkey,* ch. 6.

8. Jasper Neel detects the same problem in Plato. Plato critiques the act of writing with writing. Refer to Neel.

9. Consult Foucault; and *Students'* 2.

10. Darsie Bowden's *Mythology of Voice* provides a usable analysis of the role of expressionism in composition history.

11. To more fully appreciate the progression of African American vernacular pedagogy, consult Robert L. Williams, ed., *Ebonics: The True Language of Black Folks* (St. Louis: Williams and Assocs., 1975) and Theresa Perry and Lisa Delpit, eds., *The Real Ebonics Debate* (Boston: Beacon, 1998).

Works Cited and Consulted

Anderson, Victor. *Beyond Ontological Blackness: An Essay on African American Religious and Cultural Criticism.* New York: Continuum, 1995.

Andrews, William L., ed. *Critical Essays on Frederick Douglass.* Boston: Hall, 1991.

———. Introduction. Chesnutt, *Collected.*

———. *The Literary Career of Charles W. Chesnutt.* Baton Rouge: Louisiana State UP, 1980.

———. "*My Bondage and My Freedom* and the American Literary Renaissance of the 1850s." Andrews, *Critical* 133–47.

Appiah, Kwame Anthony. "The Conservation of 'Races.'" *Black American Literature Forum* 23.1 (1989): 37–60.

———. "The Uncompleted Argument: Du Bois and the Illusion of Race." Gates, "*Race*" 21–37.

Asante, Molefi. *The Afrocentric Idea.* Philadelphia: Temple UP, 1987.

Bacon, Jacqueline, and Glen McClish. "Reinventing the Master's Tools: Nineteenth-Century African American Literary Societies of Philadelphia and Rhetorical Education." *Rhetoric Society Quarterly* 30.4 (2000): 19–47.

Baker, Houston A. *Blues, Ideology, and Afro-American Literature: A Vernacular Theory.* Chicago: U of Chicago P, 1984.

———. *Long Black Song: Essays in Black American Literature and Culture.* Charlottesville: UP of Virginia, 1972.

———. *Modernism and the Harlem Renaissance.* Chicago: U of Chicago P, 1987.

Bakhtin, M. M. *The Dialogic Imagination.* Austin: U of Texas, 1981.

Baldwin, James. *Another Country.* New York: Dial, 1962.

Baraka, Imamu. *Raise Race Rays Raze: Essays since 1965.* New York: Vintage, 1972.

Berlin, James A. *Rhetoric and Reality: Writing Instruction in American Colleges, 1900–1985.* Carbondale: Southern Illinois UP, 1987.

———. *Writing Instruction in Nineteenth-Century American Colleges.* Carbondale: Southern Illinois UP, 1984.

Bingham, Caleb. *The Columbian Orator.* 1st Vermont ed. Middlebury: William Slade, 1816.

Blassingame, John. *The Frederick Douglass Papers.* Vol. 1. New Haven: Yale UP, 1979.

Boas, Franz. *Anthropology and Modern Life.* New York: Norton, 1962.

————. *The Mind of Primitive Man*. New York: Free, 1938.

Bowden, Darsie. *The Mythology of Voice*. Portsmouth: Boynton/Cook, 1999.

Braithwaite, William Stanley. "The Negro in American Literature." 1925. Rpt. in Mitchell 32–44.

Brodhead, Richard H. Introduction. Chesnutt, *Conjure* 1–21.

————, ed. *The Journals of Charles Chesnutt*. Durham, NC: Duke UP, 1993.

Brodie, Fawn M. *No Man Knows My History: The Life of Joseph Smith*. New York: Vintage, 1971.

————. *Thomas Jefferson: An Intimate History*. New York: Bantam, 1975.

Brooks, Charlotte K., ed. *Tapping Potential: English and Language Arts for the Black Learner*. Urbana, IL: NCTE, 1985.

Brooks, Cleanth. *The Language of the American South*. Athens: U of Georgia P, 1985.

Brown, Sterling A., Arthur P. Davis, and Ulysses Lee, eds. *The Negro Caravan*. New York: Dryden, 1941.

Bruch, Patrick, and Richard Marback. "Race, Literacy, and the Value of Rights Rhetoric." *CCC* 53.4 (2002): 651–74.

Burke, Kenneth. *Counter-Statement*. Berkeley: U of California P, 1931.

Burstein, Andrew. *The Inner Jefferson: Portrait of a Grieving Optimist*. Charlottesville: UP of Virginia, 1991.

Byerman, Keith E. *Seizing the Word: History, Art, and Self in the Works of W. E. B. Du Bois*. Athens: U of Georgia P, 1994.

Callahan, John F. *In the African-American Grain: The Pursuit of Voice in Twentieth Century Black Fiction*. Urbana: U of Illinois P, 1988.

Campbell, Kermit Ernest. "'Real Niggaz's Don't Die': African American Students Speaking Themselves into Their Writing." Severino, Guerra, and Butler 67–78.

Carby, Hazel V. Foreword. *Seraph on the Suwanee*. New York: Scribner's, 1948. Ed. Henry Louis Gates Jr. New York: Harper, 1991.

Chesnutt, Charles. *Collected Stories of Charles Chesnutt*. Ed. William L. Andrews. New York: Mentor, 1992.

————. *The Conjure Woman and Other Conjure Tales*. Ed. Richard H. Brodhead. Durham, NC: Duke UP, 1993. Rpt. from *The Conjure Woman*. New York: Houghton, 1899.

————. *The House Behind the Cedars*. New York: Houghton, 1900. Ed. Donald B. Gibson. New York: Penguin, 1993.

————. *The Journals of Charles W. Chesnutt*. Ed. Richard H. Brodhead. Durham, NC: Duke UP, 1993.

Christian, Barbara. "The Race for Theory." *Cultural Critique* 6 (1987). Rpt. in Mitchell 348–59.

Comfort, Juanita Rodgers. "Becoming a Writerly Self: Engaging Black Feminist Essays." *CCC* 51.4 (2000): 540–59.

Crummell, Alexander. *Destiny and Race: Selected Writings of Alexander Crummell, 1840–1898*. Ed. William Jeremiah Moses. Amherst: U of Massachusetts P, 1992.

Darwin, Charles. *The Origin of the Species*. New York: Books, Inc., 1859.

Davis, Charles T. *Black Is the Color of the Cosmos: Essays on Afro-American*

Literature and Culture, 1942–1981. Ed. Henry Louis Gates Jr. Washington, DC: Howard UP, 1989.

Davis, F. James. *Who Is Black?: One Nation's Definition*. University Park: Pennsylvania State UP, 1991.

Davis, Thadious M. *Nella Larsen: Novelist of the Harlem Renaissance*. Baton Rouge: Louisiana State UP, 1994.

Dillard, J. L. *Black English: Its History and Usage in the United States*. New York: Vintage, 1973.

Douglas, Ann. *Terrible Honesty: Mongrel Manhattan in the 1920s*. New York: Farrar, 1995.

Douglass, Frederick. "The Heroic Slave." 1853. Rpt. in *Three Classic African-American Novels*. Ed. William L. Andrews. New York: Mentor, 1990. 25–69.

———. *The Life and Times of Frederick Douglass*. Hartford: Park, 1881.

———. *My Bondage and My Freedom*. New York: Miller, Oration, and Mulligan, 1855.

———. *Narrative of the Life of Frederick Douglass, an American Slave. Written by Himself*. Boston: Anti-Slavery Office, 1845. Rpt. in *The Classic Slave Narratives*. Ed. Henry Louis Gates Jr. New York: Mentor, 1987. 245–331.

Du Bois, W. E. B. *Against Racism: Unpublished Essays, Papers, Addresses, 1887–1961*. Ed. Herbert Aptheker. Amherst: U of Massachusetts P, 1985.

———. *The Autobiography of W. E. B. Du Bois*. New York: International, 1968.

———. "Chesnutt." *Crisis* (Jan. 1933). Rpt. in Du Bois, *Writings* 1234.

———. "The Conservation of Races." *Occasional Papers* (American Negro Academy) No. 2 (1897). Rpt. in Du Bois, *Writings* 815–26.

———. "Criteria of Negro Art." *Crisis* (26 Oct. 1926). Rpt. in Du Bois, *Writings* 993–1002.

———. *Dark Princess*. Harcourt, 1928. Introd. Claudia Tate. Jackson: UP of Mississippi, 1995.

———. *Dusk of Dawn: An Essay Toward an Autobiography of the Race Concept*. Harcourt, 1940. Rpt. in Du Bois, *Writings* 551–802.

———. *The Quest of the Silver Fleece*. McClurg, 1911. New York: Negro UP, 1969.

———. *The Souls of Black Folk*. McClurg, 1903. Rpt. in *Three Negro Classics*. New York: Avon, 1965. 207–388.

———. *Writings*. New York: Library of America, 1986.

Elbow, Peter, ed. *Landmark Essays on Voice and Writing*. Davis, CA: Hermagoras, 1994.

———. *Writing Without Teachers*. New York: Oxford UP, 1973.

———. *Writing with Power*. New York: Oxford UP, 1981.

Ellison, Ralph. *Invisible Man*. New York: Random, 1947.

———. "The Little Man at the Chehaw Station: The American Artist and His Audience." *American Scholar* (winter 1977–78). Rpt. in *Going to the Territory*. Ed. Ralph Ellison. New York: Vintage, 1986. 3–38.

Emerson, Ralph Waldo. *English Traits*. Ed. Howard Mumford Jones. Cambridge: Harvard UP, 1966.

———. "Nature." *Essays, Poems, Addresses*. Ed. Walter J. Black. Roslyn, NY: Classic Club, 1941. 73–116.

————. *Representative Men*. Rpt. in *Ralph Waldo Emerson: Essays and Lectures*. New York: Library of America, 1983. 633–761.

————. "Self-Reliance." *Essays, Poems, Addresses*. Ed. Walter J. Black. Roslyn, NY: Classic Club, 1941. 119–46.

————. *The Works of Ralph Waldo Emerson*. Boston: Houghton, 1883.

Esonwanne, Uzo. "'Race' and Hermeneutics: Paradigm Shift--From Scientific to Hermeneutic Understanding of Race." *African American Review* 26.4 (1992): 565–82.

Evans, Henry L. "An Afrocentric Multicultural Writing Project." Severino, Guerra, and Butler 273–86.

Fauset, Jessie. *Plum Bun*. New York: Stokes, 1928. New York: Beacon, 1990.

Ferguson, SallyAnn H. "Rena Walden: Chesnutt's Failed 'Future American.'" *Southern Literary Review* 15.1 (1982): 74–82.

Fishkin, Shelley Fisher. *Was Huck Black?: Mark Twain and African-American Voices*. New York: Oxford UP, 1993.

Fishkin, Shelley Fisher, and Carla L. Peterson. "'We Hold These Truths to Be Self-Evident': The Rhetoric of Frederick Douglass's Journalism." Sundquist, *Frederick* 199–204.

Foner, Philip S., ed. *W. E. B. Du Bois Speaks: Speeches and Addresses, 1890–1919*. New York: Pathfinder, 1991.

————, ed. *W. E. B. Du Bois Speaks: Speeches and Addresses, 1920–1963*. New York: Pathfinder, 1991.

Foner, Philip S., and Robert James Branham, eds. *Lift Every Voice and Sing: African American Oratory, 1787–1900*. Tuscaloosa: U of Alabama P, 1998.

Foucault, Michel. *Power/Knowledge: Selected Interviews and Other Writings, 1972–1977*. New York: Pantheon, 1980.

Gates, Henry Louis, Jr. *Figures in Black: Words, Signs, and the "Racial" Self*. New York: Oxford UP, 1989.

————. *Loose Canons: Notes on the Culture Wars*. New York: Oxford UP, 1992.

————, ed. *"Race," Writing, and Difference*. Chicago: U of Chicago P, 1985.

————. *The Signifying Monkey: A Theory of African-American Literature*. New York: Oxford UP, 1988.

Gates, Henry Louis, Jr., and K. A. Appiah, eds. *Zora Neale Hurston: Critical Perspectives Past and Present*. New York: Amistad, 1993.

Gates, Henry Louis, Jr., and Sieglinde Lemke, eds. *The Complete Stories of Zora Neale Hurston*. New York: Harper, 1995.

Gates, Henry Louis, Jr., and Cornel West. *The Future of the Race*. New York: Knopf, 1996.

Gayle, Addison, Jr., ed. *The Black Aesthetic*. Garden City, NY: Anchor, 1972.

————. ed. *Black Expression: Essays by and about Black Americans in The Creative Arts*. New York: Weybright, 1969.

Gibson, Donald B. *The Politics of Literary Expression: A Study of Major Black Writers*. Westport, CT: Greenwood, 1981.

Giddings, Paula. *When and Where I Enter: The Impact of Black Women on Race and Sex in America*. New York: Bantam, 1984.

Gilyard, Keith. *Let's Flip the Script: An African American Discourse on Language, Literature and Learning*. Detroit: Wayne State UP, 1996.

————. *Voices of the Self: A Study of Language Competence*. Detroit: Wayne State UP, 1991.

Golden, James L., and Corbett, Edward, eds. *The Rhetoric of Blair, Campbell, and Whately.* Carbondale: Southern Illinois UP, 1990.

Gossett, Thomas F. *Race: The History of an Idea in America*. Dallas: Southern Methodist UP, 1963.

Harper, Frances E. W. *Iola Leroy*. 1892. Rpt. in *The African American Novel in the Age of Reaction*. Ed. William L. Andrews. New York: Mentor, 1992. 3–212.

————. "We Are All Bound Up Together." Rpt. in Foner and Branham 456–60.

Harper, Phillip Brian. "Nationalism and Social Division in Black Arts Poetry of the 1960s." *African American Literary Theory*. Ed. Winston Napier. New York: New York UP, 2000. 460–74.

Harris, Joel Chandler. *Uncle Remus: His Songs and His Sayings*. Spec. Ed. Norwalk, CT: Heritage, 1957.

Harris, Leonard, ed. *The Philosophy of Alain Locke: Harlem Renaissance and Beyond*. Philadelphia: Temple UP, 1989.

Heath, Shirley Brice. *Ways with Words: Language, Life, and Work in Communities and Classrooms*. New York: Cambridge UP, 1983.

Heermance, J. Noel. *Charles W. Chesnutt: America's First Black Novelist*. Hamden, CT: Arch, 1974.

Hemenway, Robert E. *Zora Neale Hurston: A Literary Biography*. Urbana: U of Illinois P, 1977.

Holloway, Karla. "The Emergent Voice: The Word Within Its Texts." Gates and Appiah 67–75.

hooks, bell. "'When I Was a Young Soldier for the Revolution': Coming to Voice." *Talking Back: Thinking Feminist, Thinking Black*. Boston: South End, 1984. Rpt. in *Landmark Essays on Voice and Writing*. Ed. Peter Elbow. Davis, CA: Hermagoras, 1994. 51–58.

Huggins, Nathan Irvin. *The Harlem Renaissance*. New York: Oxford UP, 1971.

Hughes, Langston. "The Negro Artist and the Racial Mountain." *The Nation* 122 (1926). Rpt. in Mitchell 55–59.

Hurston, Zora Neale. "Art and Such." *Reading Black, Reading Feminist: A Critical Anthology*. Ed. Henry Louis Gates, Jr. New York: Meridian, 1990. 21–26.

————. "Crazy for This Democracy." Walker 165–68.

————. *Dust Tracks on the Road*. New York: Lippincott, 1942. Ed. Henry Louis Gates Jr. New York: Harper, 1991.

————. "How It Feels to Be Colored Me." Walker 152–55.

————. *Jonah's Gourd Vine*. New York: Lippincott, 1934. Ed. Henry Louis Gates Jr. New York: Harper, 1990.

————. *Mules and Men*. New York: Lippincott, 1935. Ed. Henry Louis Gates Jr. New York: Harper, 1990.

————. *The Sanctified Church*. Berkeley: Turtle Island Found.: 1981.

————. *Seraph on the Suwanee*. New York: Scribner's, 1948. Ed. Henry Louis Gates Jr. New York: Harper, 1991.

————. *Their Eyes Were Watching God*. New York: Lippincott, 1937. Ed. Henry Louis Gates Jr. New York: Harper, 1990.

———. "What White Publishers Won't Print." Walker 169–73.

———. *Zora Neale Hurston: A Life in Letters*. Ed. Carla Kaplan. New York: Doubleday, 2001.

James, Joy. *Transcending the Talented Tenth: Black Leaders and American Intellectuals*. New York: Routledge, 1997.

Johnson, Barbara. "Thresholds of Difference: Structures of Address in Zora Neale Hurston." Gates and Appiah 130–40.

Johnson, Charles. *Being and Race: Black Writing since 1970*. Bloomington: Indiana UP, 1990.

Johnson, James Weldon. *Black Manhattan*. New York: Knopf, 1930. Introd. Kathryn Wilson. New York: Da Capo, 1991.

Jones, Gayl. *Liberating Voices: Oral Tradition in African American Literature*. New York: Penguin, 1992.

Jones, Leroi, and Larry Neal, eds. *Black Fire: An Anthology of Afro-American Writing*. New York: Morrow, 1968.

Jordan, June. "Requiem for the Champ." *Technical Difficulties: Selected Political Essays*. London: Virago P, 1992. 197–202.

Jordan, Winthrop D. *White over Black: American Attitudes Toward the Negro, 1550–1812*. New York: Norton, 1977.

Keller, Frances Richardson. *An American Crusade: The Life of Charles Waddell Chesnutt*. Provo, UT: Brigham Young UP, 1978.

Labov, William. *The Study of Nonstandard English*. Champaign, IL: NCTE, 1970.

Lampe, Gregory P. *Frederick Douglass: Freedom's Voice, 1818–1845*. East Lansing: Michigan State UP, 1998.

Larsen, Nella. *Quicksand* and *Passing*. Pub. separately by Knopf in 1928 and 1929, resp. Ed. Deborah E. McDowell. New Brunswick, NJ: Rutgers UP, 1986.

Lauter, Paul. *Canons and Contexts*. New York: Oxford UP, 1991.

Lauter, Paul, et al., eds. *The Heath Anthology of American Literature*. Vol. 1. Lexington, MA: Heath, 1990.

Lewis, David Levering. *W. E. B. Du Bois: Biography of a Race, 1868–1919*. New York: Holt, 1993.

———. *When Harlem Was in Vogue*. New York: Oxford UP, 1989.

Locke, Alain, ed. *The New Negro: Voices of the Harlem Renaissance*. New York: Boni, 1925.

———. *Race Contacts and Interracial Relations*. Washington, DC: Howard UP, 1992.

Logan, Shirley Wilson. *"We Are Coming": The Persuasive Discourse of Nineteenth-Century Black Women*. Carbondale: Southern Illinois UP, 1999.

Matthiessen, F. O. *American Renaissance: Art and Expression in the Age of Emerson and Whitman*. New York: Oxford UP, 1941.

McFeely, William S. *Frederick Douglass*. New York: Touchstone, 1991.

McKay, Nellie Y. "Jean Toomer." *African American Writers: Profiles of Their Lives and Works from the 1700s to the Present*. Ed. Valerie Smith, Lea Baechler, and A. Walton Litz. New York: Collier, 1993.

Mencken, H. L. *The American Language: An Inquiry into the Development of English in the United States*. 4th ed. New York: Knopf, 1937.

Mikell, Gwendolyn. "Feminism and Black Culture in the Ethnography of Zora Neale Hurston." *African American Pioneers in Anthropology.* Ed. Ira E. Harrison. Urbana: U of Illinois P, 1999. 52–69.

Mitchell, Angelyn, ed. *Within the Circle: An Anthology of African American Literary Criticism from the Harlem Renaissance to the Present.* Durham, NC: Duke UP, 1994.

Morrison, Toni. *Playing in the Dark: Whiteness and the Literary Imagination.* Cambridge: Harvard UP, 1992.

Moses, Wilson J. "Writing Freely? Frederick Douglass and the Constraints of Racialized Writing." Sundquist, *Frederick* 66–83.

Neal, Larry. "The Black Arts Movement." *Drama Review* 12.4 (1968). Rpt. in Mitchell 184–98.

Neel, Jasper. *Plato, Derrida, and Writing.* Carbondale: Southern Illinois UP, 1988.

North, Michael. *The Dialect of Modernism: Race, Language, and Twentieth-Century Literature.* New York: Oxford UP, 1994.

Ong, Walter. *Orality and Literacy: The Technologizing of the Word.* London: Routledge, 1988.

Powell, Malea. "Blood and Scholarship: One Mixed-Blood's Story." *Race, Rhetoric and Composition.* Portsmouth: Boynton/Cook, 1999.

Rampersad, Arnold. *The Art and Imagination of W. E. B. Du Bois.* New York: Schocken, 1976.

Reed, Ishmael. *Mumbo Jumbo.* New York: Macmillan, 1972.

Reynolds, David S. *Beneath the American Renaissance: The Subversive Imagination in the Age of Emerson and Melville.* Cambridge: Harvard UP, 1988.

Richardson, Robert D. *Emerson: The Mind on Fire.* Berkeley: U of California P, 1995.

Rickford, John Russell. *Spoken Soul: The Story of Black English.* New York: Wiley, 2000.

Royster, Jacqueline Jones. *Traces of a Stream: Literacy and Social Change among African American Women.* Pittsburgh: U of Pittsburgh P, 2000.

Rusch, Frederick L., ed. *A Jean Toomer Reader: Selected Unpublished Writings.* New York: Oxford UP, 1993.

Sandglass (newsletter). Pub. as insert to Harris. Norwalk, CT: Heritage Book Club, 1957.

Schuyler, George S. *Black No More.* New York: Macaulay, 1931. Ed. Richard Yarborough. Boston: Northeastern UP, 1989.

———. "The Negro-Art Hokum." *Nation* 122 (1926). Rpt. in Mitchell 51–54.

Segal, Erich, ed. *The Dialogues of Plato.* New York: Bantam, 1986.

Severino, Carol, Juan C. Guerra, and Johnnella E. Butler, eds. *Writing in Multicultural Settings.* New York: MLA, 1997.

Smitherman, Geneva. *Talkin and Testifyin: The Language of Black America.* Detroit: Wayne State UP, 1977.

Sowell, Thomas. *Civil Rights: Rhetoric or Reality?* New York: Morrow, 1984.

Stanton, William. *The Leopard's Spots: Scientific Attitudes Toward Race in America, 1815–1859.* Chicago: U of Chicago P, 1960.

Students' Right to Their Own Language. Spec. issue of CCC 25 (1974): 1–32.

Stull, Bradford T. *Amid the Fall, Dreaming of Eden*. Carbondale: Southern Illinois UP, 1999.

Sundquist, Eric J., ed. *Frederick Douglass: New Literary and Historical Essays*. New York: Cambridge UP, 1990.

———. *To Wake the Nations: Race in the Making of American Literature*. Cambridge: Harvard UP, 1993.

Walker, Alice, ed. *I Love Myself When I Am Laughing . . . and Then Again When I Am Looking Mean and Impressive*. New York: Feminist, 1979.

Wall, Cheryl. "Zora Neale Hurston: Changing Her Own Words." Gates and Appiah 76–97.

Washington, Mary Helen. "Zora Neale Hurston: A Woman in Half Shadow." Walker 7–25.

Wideman, John Edgar. "Charles Chesnutt and the WPA Narratives: The Oral and Written Roots of Afro-American Literature." *The Slaves Narrative*. Ed. Charles T. Davis and Henry Louis Gates, Jr. New York: Oxford UP, 59–78.

Winterowd, W. Ross. *Contemporary Rhetoric: A Conceptual Background with Readings*. San Diego: Harcourt, 1973.

———. *The Rhetoric of the "Other" Literature*. Carbondale: Southern Illinois UP, 1990.

Wolfe, George C. *The Colored Museum*. New York: Grove, 1985.

Wright, Richard. "Blueprint for Negro Writing." *New Challenge* 11 (1937). Rpt. in Mitchell 97–106.

Yarborough, Richard. "Race, Violence, and Manhood: The Masculine Idea in Frederick Douglass's 'The Heroic Slave.'" Sundquist, *Frederick* 166–88.

Zack, Naomi. *Race and Mixed Race*. Philadelphia: Temple UP, 1993.

Zamir, Shamoon. *Dark Voices: W. E. B. Du Bois and American Thought, 1888–1903*. Chicago: U of Chicago P, 1995.

Index

Goodness, Truth, and Beauty, discussion of, 73–74
"Goophered Grapevine, The" (Chesnutt), 46–49, 59–61
Gorgias (Plato), 3, 4
Gossett, Thomas, 26
Grant, Madison, 39
Grant, Tom *(The Heroic Slave)*, 17–18
"Gray Wolf's Ha'nt" (Chesnutt), 57, 59
Great Barrington, Massachusetts, 63–64, 65
Great Migration, 36
Greece, ancient, 58
Gresham *(Iola Leroy)*, 22
Griffiths, Julia: *Autographs of Freedom,* 10

Hamlet, 19
Harlem Renaissance, 46, 73, 77, 84, 93; Hughes and, 40–42; Larsen and, 42–43; Locke and, 37–40; New Black Aesthetic and, 97, 98; one-drop rule and, 31–34; Schuyler and, 35–37
Harper, Frances E. W., 8, 20–24; Douglass and, 20, 22, 24; *Iola Leroy,* 21–22
Harper, Phillip Brian, 96
Harris, Joel Chandler, 52–55, 57, 60, 86, 111; *Uncle Remus: His Songs and Sayings,* 53, 54; *Uncle Remus Tales,* 53, 56
Harvard University, 66
Heath, Shirley Brice, 102
Heermance, J. Noel, 49
Hemenway, Robert, 73, 84
Henry, Patrick, 16
hermeneutic and race, 44–45, 109
Heroic Slave, The (Douglass), 10, 16–19
"Her Virginia Mammy" (Chesnutt), 51
heteroglossia, 12–13, 109
Hohfelder, Clara ("Her Virginia Mammy"), 51
Holloway, Karla, 90

homophobia, 96
hoodoo and voodoo, 75, 86, 87
"Hoodoo" (Hurston), 86
hooks, bell: *When I Was a Young Soldier for the Revolution,* 24
Howard University, 85
Howells, William Dean, 49
"How It Feels to Be Colored Me" (Hurston), 76–78
Huggins, Nathan I., 71
Hughes, Langston, 41, 42, 84, 91; *Mule Bone* (with Hurston), 84; "The Negro Artist and the Racial Mountain," 40
Hurston, Zora Neale, 74–91, 93, 98; African-American culture and, 87–91; ethnography and, 85–87; gender and, 75, 83–85
Hurston, Zora Neale, works of: "Art and Such," 78–80, 82; "The Characteristics of Negro Expression," 89, 91; *Dust Tracks on the Road,* 81, 89; "Folk Tales," 86; "The Gilded Six Bits," 88; "Hoodoo," 86; "How It Feels to Be Colored Me," 76–78; *Jonah's Gourd Vine,* 89; *Mule Bone* (with Hughes), 84; *Mules and Men,* 75, 86, 89, 90; "My People, My People," 81; "Race Leader," 78–79; *Seraph on the Sewanee,* 90–91; *Their Eyes Were Watching God,* 76; "What White Publishers Won't Print," 82–83

Icelandic Sagas, 58
identity, 2, 23, 94, 97, 99, 106; American, 96; civilization and, 62; gender and, 42; mixed race and, 50, 57. *See also* racial identity
idiom, 89, 90
imagery in expression, 89
I-narrators, 1
intraracism, 50, 52
intratextuality, 63
Invisible Man (Ellison), 96
Iola Leroy (Harper), 21–22

David G. Holmes is an associate professor of English and the director of the English composition program at Pepperdine University. A 1995 recipient of the Scholars for the Dream Award, he has had some of his essays published in the *CLA Journal*, the *Journal of Teaching Writing*, and the anthology *Race, Rhetoric, and Composition*, edited by Keith Gilyard. Holmes's current research projects include the rhetoric of the civil rights movement mass meetings and the racial aesthetics of Carl Van Vechten.

Printed in the United States
30223LVS00001B/124-180

9 780809 325474